THE
BIRD FEEDER
BOOK

By Donald and Lillian Stokes

GORDON MORRISON

Also by Donald and Lillian Stokes

Stokes Nature Guides,
which include:

A Guide to Nature in Winter
A Guide to Bird Behavior, Volume I
A Guide to Bird Behavior, Volume II
A Guide to Observing Insect Lives
A Guide to Enjoying Wildflowers
A Guide to Animal Tracking and Behavior

Also by Donald Stokes

The Natural History of Wild Shrubs and Vines

THE
BIRD FEEDER BOOK

AN EASY GUIDE TO ATTRACTING, IDENTIFYING, AND UNDERSTANDING YOUR FEEDER BIRDS

Donald and Lillian Stokes

Authors of *Stokes Nature Guides*

Illustration of feeders by Gordon Morrison

Range maps by Leslie Cowperthwaite

LITTLE, BROWN AND COMPANY
Boston   Toronto

9   8   7   6   5   4   3

Library of Congress Cataloging-in-Publication Data

Stokes, Donald W.
    The bird feeder book.

    Bibliography: p. 84
    1. Birds, Attracting of. 2. Bird feeders — Design and construc-
tion. 3. Birds — United States. I. Stokes, Lillian Q. II. Title.
QL676.5.S87 1987   598'.07'23473   87-3016
ISBN 0-316-81733-3

Photograph Acknowledgments

Animals/Animals: A. Reinhold — 13; R. Richardson — 19.
Aspects: 7 bottom.
The Brown Company: 3 top left.
Cornell Laboratory of Ornithology: R. and D. Aitkenhead — 52 right;
    W. C. Bloomer — 78; L. B. Chapman — 35; L. Elliot — 61 right; J. R.
    Harris — 55 bottom; M. Hopiak — 23, 25, 32, 42, 45 top, 50, 51, 55
    top, 57, 59 bottom, 62, 63 right, 69, 72 top; H. Mayfield — 77; J.
    Sanford — 11; J. Smith — 75; D.P.H. Watson — 74; J. Weissinger
    — 70, 71; T. Willcox — 39 left/right, 81; J. R. Woodward — 27, 30
    left, 31, 33, 40, 41, 43, 45 bottom, 56, 63 left, 67, 72 bottom, 73 top,
    79, 83.
Droll Yankees, Inc.: vi, 3 left/right in first column.
Hyde Bird Feeder Company: 3 top right.
Photo Researchers, Inc.: J. Bova — 59 top; K. and D. Dannen — 37; R.
    Kline — 30 right; C. Larsen — 21; L. L. Rue III — 73 bottom.
D. and L. Stokes: 5, 7, 9, 16.
VIREO: A. Cruickshank — 48, 61 left, 65, 68; C. H. Greenwalt — 44, 52
    left, 53 top/bottom; O. S. Pettingill, Jr. — 47; F. K. Schleicher — 15;
    J. Stasz — 82; R. Villani — 49.

Illustration on p. i Copyright ©
1987 by Gordon Morrison.

WAK

Designed by Patricia Dunbar

Published simultaneously in Canada
by Little, Brown & Company (Canada) Limited

PRINTED IN UNITED STATES OF AMERICA

CONTENTS

ATTRACTING BIRDS   **1**

The Four Basic Feeders   1

Sunflower Seed Feeder   2

Ground Feeder with Cracked Corn
and Mixed Seed   4

Suet Feeder   6

Water   8

How to Attract Hummingbirds   10

Dealing with Squirrels   12

Troubleshooting   14

Plantings That Attract Birds   16

BIRD BEHAVIOR   **18**

Watching Bird Behavior   18

Social Behavior   20

Maintenance Behavior   22

A Year in the Life of a Bird   24

Four Behaviors Everyone Asks About   26

THE BIRDS   **28**

Identifying Your Birds   28

Cardinal   30

Chickadees   32

Cowbird   34

American Crow   36

Evening Grosbeak   38

Finches   40

Goldfinch   44

Grackle   46

House Sparrow   48

Hummingbirds   50

Jays   54

Junco   56

Mockingbird   58

Mourning Dove   60

Nuthatches   62

Pigeon   64

Pine Siskin   66

Red-Winged Blackbird   68

Sparrows   70

Starling   74

Titmouse   76

Towhee   78

Woodpeckers   80

Resources   84

Your Bird Feeder Journal   86

ATTRACTING BIRDS

The joy of attracting birds is open to everyone and is remarkably easy if certain basic guidelines are followed. Birds need food, water, shelter from predators, and places to raise their young. Provide birds with the foods they love and with the kinds of flowers, shrubs, and trees that create an attractive habitat, and wild birds will flock to your property.

Over the years we have had success in attracting more than one hundred species of birds to our yard and have had more than forty species nest there. In the following pages we share our recommendations on how to meet the needs of birds in some of the best and easiest ways.

THE FOUR BASIC FEEDERS

The most important factor in setting up a successful feeding station, is to offer a variety of foods and to place each in the proper setting. Through years of experience and research, we have found that a good all-around feeding program which will attract the most birds throughout the year must include at least four things:

1. A hanging feeder with sunflower seed
2. A ground or tray-type feeder with cracked corn and mixed seed
3. Suet feeder
4. Water

On the next few pages are detailed descriptions of each type of feeder and suggestions on how to make them even more attractive to birds.

Tube feeder with sunflower seed; male cardinal, black-capped chickadee, American goldfinches, and female purple finch are enjoying a meal.

SUNFLOWER SEED FEEDER

Description: A hanging or pole-mounted feeder that contains *only* sunflower seed, desirable because sunflower seed is the *number-one* choice of most songbirds.

Birds Attracted to Sunflower Feeders: Black-capped chickadee, Carolina chickadee, tufted titmouse, white-breasted nuthatch, red-breasted nuthatch, cardinal, American goldfinch, purple finch, house finch, pine siskin, downy woodpecker, hairy woodpecker, red-bellied woodpecker, red-headed woodpecker, common flicker, evening grosbeak, starling, house sparrow, blue jay, scrub jay.

Placement of Feeder: If you are just starting, place the feeder away from the house in an area that you can see but that is also near trees or shrubs visited by birds. Birds feel safer and are less hesitant to come to a feeder if vegetation is nearby. Once they are used to the feeder, you can gradually try moving it closer to your house for better viewing. Put it near the windows you look out of most often. You want to be sure not to miss any exciting behavior, and you will be amazed at how much is happening once you start looking.

You can hang the feeder from a tree, mount it on a pole, or hang it from a wire strung between two supports. You *must* use baffles on the feeder to keep away squirrels. See the chapter "Dealing with Squirrels," p. 12.

How soon the birds discover and start using your feeder depends on many things, such as where you live, whether there is a good bird population in your area, and whether some of the birds are already familiar with feeders. Be patient and they will soon arrive.

Types of Sunflower Seed: There are three kinds of sunflower seed available, distinguished by size and the pattern on their hulls. Gray-striped seed is the largest; next is the medium-sized black-striped sunflower; and the smallest is black oil sunflower, which has all-black hulls. All of these are very popular with birds, but a recent study by Dr. Aelred Geis of the U.S. Fish and Wildlife Service showed that the black oil sunflower is the preferred type of most seed-eating birds. It has a thinner shell that is easier for small birds to remove and has a higher percentage of oil for its weight.

Sunflower seed is also available with the shells already removed; this is called hulled sunflower or sunflower hearts. It is somewhat more expensive than the unhulled varieties, but it is highly attractive to many species of birds, including woodpeckers. Dr. Geis's study found that it is the number-one choice of the American goldfinch, even preferred over thistle (niger) seed. An added advantage is that there are no empty hulls to clean up under the feeder.

CHOOSING A SUNFLOWER FEEDER

If you walk into any store with bird feeders, you will be greeted with a bewildering array of choices. This section will help you choose the best ones. We recommend that you invest your money in a well-made feeder in the beginning, for it will last a long time and will reward you with years of enjoyment.

Here are some overall features to consider when buying any bird feeder:

— It should be easy to fill
— It should hold lots of seed so you don't have to fill it as often
— It should be easy to take apart and clean
— Clear parts should be plastic and not glass (preferably Lexan brand plastic, which is unbreakable and cannot be chewed by squirrels)
— It should protect the seed from rain and snow

— It should have metal perches and reinforced openings if it is a tube feeder, so squirrels cannot chew them
— It should have a manufacturer's guarantee if possible

Types of Feeders

Below are examples of some types of bird feeders that are available, with recommendations based on our own experiences.

Bowl-with-baffle Feeder (above left). Advantages: Holds lots of seed; protects seed from weather; displays seed clearly to birds; enables birds to cling underneath or perch inside; accommodates many birds at once; is easy to fill and clean; comes with adjustable squirrel baffle. Example shown is the Droll Yankees, Inc., Big Top.

Tube Feeder (above right). Advantages: Is easy to fill; has metal-reinforced perches and holes that are squirrel-resistant; displays seed clearly to birds; large models hold lots of seed; allows options of attaching a tray underneath to catch scattered seed and/or a dome-like squirrel baffle above. Examples shown are Droll Yankees, Inc., models A-6 (left) and B-7(right).

Audubon Feeder (top left). Advantages: Hanging model holds more seed than most other feeders, 2.2 gallons (10 pounds); is easy to fill and clean; displays seed clearly; releases seed from all perches until feeder is empty. Comes in hanging or pole-mounted models with squirrel baffle. This feeder is made by The Brown Company.

House Hopper-type Feeder (above right). Advantages: Has an attractive rustic look; larger models hold large quantity of seed; allows several birds to perch at once. Make sure the model you get is easy to fill, and use with a baffle to keep squirrels away. Example shown is the Hyde Company's Deluxe Filling Station.

Window Feeder (above). Advantages: Brings birds up close to your window for exciting views. Example shown is from Aspects, a company that makes feeders.

See the chapter "Resources," p. 84, for a list of other bird feeder and birdseed companies.

GROUND FEEDER WITH CRACKED CORN AND MIXED SEED

Description: Cracked corn and mixed seed scattered directly on the ground or on a tray-type feeder.

Birds Attracted by Ground Feeders: Cardinal, dark-eyed junco, white-throated sparrow, white-crowned sparrow, fox sparrow, American tree sparrow, song sparrow, mourning dove, pigeon, tufted titmouse, black-capped chickadee, blue jay, scrub jay, crow, house sparrow, starling, brown-headed cowbird, common grackle, red-winged blackbird, rufous-sided towhee, ring-necked pheasant, northern bobwhite.

Creating a Ground Feeder: To create a ground feeder that accommodates the most birds, scatter seed directly on the ground or place the seed on an elevated feeding tray. A hopper-type feeder, either hung or pole-mounted and filled with cracked corn and mixed seed, will also attract some of these birds, but its small feeding space limits the number of birds.

Sprinkle the seed over a fairly large area (our ground feeder is an 8-foot circular area) so that large flocks of birds can feed all at once. Also make your ground feeder near cover, such as a brush pile or evergreen shrubs. This allows birds to dive into cover if a predator, such as a hawk, appears. Many birds also have a pecking order in their flocks, and nearby shrubs provide a place for subordinate birds to wait while more dominant birds feed.

Types of Seed to Use: The main type of seed to use at a ground feeder is cracked corn. It is inexpensive and appeals to many ground-feeding birds. Cracked corn is sometimes available in a grade called finely cracked; choose this when possible, because more birds prefer it.

We also sprinkle some mixed seed on the ground, along with the cracked corn. We look for mixed seed that contains a high percentage of white proso mil-let, a small round whitish seed that is highly desirable to ground-feeding species like sparrows and mourning doves.

When buying mixed seed, read the labels. Beware of bargain mixes that contain seeds that birds won't eat. Buy mixes that contain these desirable seeds: sunflower, white proso millet, peanut hearts, cracked corn, and safflower. Avoid seed mixes that contain these undesirable seeds: milo, wheat, oats, rye, or rice.

Another suggestion is to buy seeds separately and make your own mix. We make a mixture of 4 parts cracked corn, 1 part white proso millet, and 1 part sunflower.

Advantages of Ground Feeders: By having a ground feeder, you can attract additional kinds and greater numbers of birds. This is because many birds, especially cardinals, juncos, towhees, and sparrows, naturally prefer to feed on or near the ground. In addition, other birds that visit hanging feeders occasionally go to the ground to feed.

Another advantage to a ground feeder is that it provides a spacious arena for you to see many fascinating features of bird behavior that do not occur at hanging feeders because of their smaller size. At our ground feeder we frequently have a flock of up to thirty juncos and tree sparrows that we see chasing and displaying, indicating their pecking orders. Mourning dove males coo and hop after females in early spring when they are courting. It is our cardinals' favorite place to do mate-feeding, their courtship ritual in which the male takes a piece of cracked corn, hops over to the female, and gently places it in her mouth.

Squirrels and some of the larger birds will come to this feeder as well, but we consider this an advantage, since they are kept busy eating the inexpensive cracked corn and are diverted from the more expensive sunflower seed offered at the hanging feeders.

Examples of ground
feeders.

BIRD-FEEDING TIPS

— Buy birdseed in large quantities; it is less expensive that way.

— Store seed in clean, dry, covered containers such as metal trash cans. If you keep these outside, lock their lids to prevent raccoons from getting at the seed.

— Use a two-quart plastic pitcher to scoop up seed and pour it into your feeder.

— Clean feeders regularly by thoroughly scrubbing with hot water and detergent. Dispose of any old or moldy food at *all* feeders, including ground feeders, to avoid possible harm to the birds.

SUET FEEDER

Description: Suet in a wire or nylon mesh container either hung or attached to a tree trunk.

Birds Attracted to Suet Feeders: Downy woodpecker, hairy woodpecker, red-bellied woodpecker, redheaded woodpecker, black-capped chickadee, Carolina chickadee, tufted titmouse, white-breasted nuthatch, red-breasted nuthatch, starling, mockingbird.

Creating a Suet Feeder: Suet is a high-energy food source for birds and is a favorite food of woodpeckers. To create a suet feeder, all you have to do is buy suet and place it in a container of some kind that the birds can easily fly to. Suet feeders can be hung from a tree, the eaves of a house, or another feeder; they can also be attached to the trunk of a tree.

Types of Suet: Beef suet is a hard type of fat that is found near the beef kidneys and loins. It is available at the meat counter of your supermarket. In the colder months, you can use it as is right from the store. In hot weather suet melts, and it is better to use commercially available suet cakes, which are rendered and thus harder.

You can render suet yourself by cutting it into small pieces, or putting it through a meat grinder, melting it in a pan with a little water, and letting it cool in muffin tins. You can create your own recipes by adding mixed seed, chopped nuts, or other ingredients to these cakes.

A Homemade Treat. Here is a recipe that appeals to the same species of birds that like suet. This mixture has proved irresistible to our titmice and is good in all seasons.

In a blender or food processor, combine 1 part peanut butter, 1 part Crisco or similar vegetable

---

ADDITIONAL WAYS TO ATTRACT BIRDS

As you gain experience in feeding birds, you might want to add some new elements such as offering fruit, baked goods, or chopped nutmeats, or putting up more feeders. Orioles and tanagers are attracted to orange halves, which you can place on a tray or nail to a tree. Some people set up thistle feeders to attract finches. Thistle is actually niger seed, which comes from Ethiopia and India and is not related to our common wildflower thistle. It is a very expensive seed, but finches enjoy it. If you are already feeding hulled sunflower, you should be attracting finches. If not, you may want to try offering thistle. You need to buy a special type of feeder with tiny holes, since this is a very small seed.

Examples of suet feeders.

shortening, 3 parts yellow cornmeal, 1 part white or whole wheat flour, and 1 part finely cracked corn. If it is too sticky, add more cornmeal or flour to make it manageable. Keep any extra in a plastic bag in the refrigerator.

This mixture can be offered in a small hanging log drilled with holes or in a small tray; it can even be smeared on a tree trunk. In the winter we stuff it into pine cones, roll them in mixed seed, and hang them on our outdoor Christmas tree for the birds. Juncos and mockingbirds love these cones.

Types of Suet Containers: There are several types of containers in which you can offer suet.

Wire Cage. This is a box of plastic-coated wire mesh in which you place the suet. It lasts a long time, is attractive, and is easy to fill with all shapes of suet pieces.

Onion Bag. These are plastic bags in which onions are often sold. They cost nothing and can be easily replaced when they wear out.

Suet Log. This is a log about 2 inches in diameter and about 1½ feet long with a hook at the top and several 1-inch-diameter holes. You can hammer or press cold suet into the holes. Since birds are used to feeding on tree trunks, this feeder mimics their natural environment.

WATER

Description: Any shallow container holding water that is placed on or above the ground.

Birds Attracted to Water: All birds need water both for drinking and bathing; therefore, all the birds that normally visit your feeder may come to your water, plus you will attract many other species such as robins, thrushes, vireos, orioles, and warblers.

Creating a Birdbath: Creating a birdbath can be as simple or complex as you wish. One of the easiest baths we have found is an aluminum trash can lid turned upside down. We place several flat stones in it so the birds can gradually wade in the water. Some people construct their own bath out of concrete or even make a series of small pools with water flowing from one to the other. There are many kinds of attractive birdbaths sold at stores. When buying one, keep in mind that it should have a gradual slope that is not slippery and that it should be no more than 3 inches deep. Small songbirds do not like water deeper than this. Ceramic baths are attractive, but if water freezes in them in winter, they could crack.

Water can be placed in a variety of situations, but it is always good to locate it near your feeders so the birds see it as they come and go. Perches near the water will make the site more attractive to the birds. We have a birdbath on a second-floor deck with a large branch tied nearby. The goldfinches love this birdbath and line up on the branch, waiting their turn.

The sound of running water is a magnet to many birds. You can make your birdbath even more appealing if you provide this. Let water drip from a

WHEN TO FEED BIRDS

The best time to begin feeding birds is in early fall, when birds are searching for reliable food supplies and will remain where they find them. Chickadee and junco flocks form in the fall and stay in a fixed area that will encompass good feeding spots.

Once you begin a feeding program, do not stop abruptly in winter. If you must be away, gradually taper off your feeding, so the birds have time to find other food sources. Better yet, have a friend or neighbor fill your feeders while you are gone.

Do not fear that birds will eat only at your feeder and forget how to feed on their own. Birds are very resourceful and will continually explore, eating a wide variety of wild foods. Follow them away from your feeder sometime and you will see for yourself.

Many people stop feeding birds in spring, when insects, seeds, and other wild foods again become abundant. However, it is perfectly fine to feed birds year-round. We do, and we have the added enjoyment of seeing them court and breed as well as bring their new fledglings to the feeders.

Example of a birdbath.

bucket that has a tiny hole in the bottom and that is suspended above the birdbath or try one of the commercial mist fountains or drip hoses made for birdbaths and garden pools.

Birds need water all year, including winter, which can be a time of drought for them. In cold climates many birds eat snow. You can keep water open at your birdbath by adding warm water, although this can mean frequent trips. We use one of the commercially available birdbath water heaters. They do not use much electricity, do not harm the birds, and keep the water just above freezing.

HOW TO ATTRACT HUMMINGBIRDS

We are always thrilled when the hummingbirds return to our yard each year. We have found that the very best way to attract hummingbirds is to grow a profusion of flowers that they like, especially red, tubular flowers. Hummingbirds drink the nectar from the flowers and feed on tiny insects they find inside. Put out hummingbird feeders as well, placing them at first near the flowers, where the hummingbirds are feeding; once the birds are accustomed to using them, you can move them closer to your house for better views. Do not be discouraged if it takes a while for the hummingbirds to use your feeders — some people have immediate success, but for others it takes longer.

Hummingbird Flowers

Hummingbirds are most often attracted to red, tubular flowers, although they also visit flowers of other colors. In our yard the flower that has been most irresistible to hummingbirds is cardinal flower, *Lobelia cardinalis*. This is a perennial that thrives in moist, rich soil in sun or part shade and requires mulching in the winter. It blooms from July through September and grows 3 feet high with spikes of gorgeous crimson flowers. It seems as if the minute the first blossom opens, there is a hummingbird waiting. It is the only flower in our garden that hummingbirds actually fight over, and other observers have reported the same thing to us.

For maximum effect, we encourage you to plant a variety of flowers, placing taller ones behind smaller ones. Following is a sample list of annuals, perennials, vines, and shrubs that are attractive to hummingbirds. Hummingbirds are also drawn to many kinds of flowering trees, such as horse chestnuts, flowering quince, mimosa, and citrus trees. For extensive lists of hummingbird plants, see reference works listed in the chapter "Resources," p. 84.

Hummingbird Feeders

There are many quality hummingbird feeders on the market. When buying one, make sure you can take it apart and reach all parts of the interior for thorough cleaning. Some people make their own hummingbird feeders by covering a small glass vial or jar with red ribbon or paint so that it resembles a red flower.

Put your feeders up in the early spring when the hummingbirds are just arriving so they will find you and want to remain in the area. You can take the feeders down after the last stragglers have migrated through.

Hummingbird Mixture

To make a syrup that will draw hummingbirds, mix 1 part white sugar with 4 parts water and boil for 1 to 2 minutes. Boiling will retard fermentation of the mixture. Cool the mixture and place it in the feeders, storing the unused portion in the refrigerator. Never use honey in place of sugar, because it rapidly ferments in the sun and grows a mold that can be fatal to hummingbirds.

Some people add red food coloring to the solution, either to attract the birds or so they can more easily see the fluid level in the feeders and know when they need refilling. We prefer not to add coloring, since most feeders have red on them anyway.

Sugar-water solutions do not provide a balanced diet for hummingbirds, but hummingbirds do not use feeders exclusively; they get their other nutrients from natural nectar and insects. Do not be surprised if hummingbirds suddenly desert your feeders. Often when there is a peak bloom of favorite hummingbird flowers — such as wild honeysuckle, trumpet vine, and mimosa — in an area, hummingbirds temporarily leave feeders.

You should thoroughly clean the feeders and replace the solution every three to four days. Scrub

Hummingbird Plants

Common Name	Scientific Name
Annuals	
Flowering tobacco	*Nicotiana* spp.*
Fuchsia	*Fuchsia* spp.
Geranium	*Pelargonium* spp.
Gladiolus	*Gladiolus* spp.
Impatiens, patient lucy, busy lizzie	*Impatiens* spp.
Lantana	*Lantana camara*
Nasturtium	*Tropaeolum majus*
Petunia	*Petunia* spp.
Pinks, sweet william	*Dianthus* spp.
Sage	*Salvia* spp.
Spiderflower	*Cleome* spp.
Perennials	
Bee balm	*Monarda* spp.
Columbine	*Aquilegia* spp.
Coralbells	*Heuchera sanguinea*
Day lily	*Hemerocallis* spp.
Hollyhock	*Althea* spp.
Larkspur	*Delphinium* spp.
Lily	*Lilium* spp.
Lupine	*Lupinus* spp.
Phlox	*Phlox* spp.
Vines	
Trumpet honeysuckle	*Lonicera sempervirens*
Trumpet vine	*Campsis radicans*
Shrubs	
Azalea	*Rhododendron* spp.
Beauty bush	*Kolkwitzia amabilis*
Butterfly bush	*Buddleia* spp.
Japanese honeysuckle	*Lonicera japonica*
Rose mallow	*Hibiscus* spp.
Scarlet bush	*Hamelia erecta*

* *Spp.* is the abbreviation for the plural of *species* and means here that more than one species is available.

A beautiful female rufous hummingbird at a good hummingbird feeder filled with sugar water. A bee guard at the opening of the feeder keeps bees away.

Other Visitors at Feeders

Ants, wasps, and bees will also be attracted to the sugar-water solution. To control ants, hang feeders from thin, monofilament fishing line. Some people also put Vaseline on the wire from which the feeder hangs. Others wrap flypaper around the branch or stake to which the feeder is attached. To control bees and wasps, put Vaseline, mineral oil, or salad oil around the feeder opening, rubbing just a little of it on the feeder hole with your finger. Bees and wasps will find the opening too slippery and will be unable to get a leg hold. Certain feeders come with their own "bee guard," a screen-like device that fits over the feeder hole. Some people have found these useful and others have not, so you may just have to experiment.

Many other species of birds have been known to come to hummingbird feeders, including orioles, tanagers, warblers, and sapsuckers. Many people are thrilled to attract these additional species. If the feeder becomes too crowded, you might try setting up several different feeders to reduce competition.

feeders with hot water and vinegar and rinse them. It is very important to maintain clean feeders, since fungi or bacteria can build up in the feeders, causing the solution to ferment or go sour.

DEALING WITH SQUIRRELS

If you put up a feeder in an area with squirrels, they will probably be attracted to it; after all, you are offering a free meal, and squirrels assume it is intended for them. Some people get so obsessed with keeping squirrels away that bird feeding becomes an unpleasant experience for them. They forget to enjoy the beauty of the wildlife they have attracted.

Our philosophy about squirrels is to do the best we can to keep them from disturbing the birds as they feed and then to enjoy them for their own equally fascinating behavior. We try to prevent them from getting to our sunflower feeders, because the seed is expensive and intended for the smaller songbirds. At the same time, we don't mind if they eat the cracked corn we offer at our ground feeder, for it is inexpensive and keeps them away from the sunflower seed. What follow are suggestions on how to protect your feeders and enjoy your squirrels at the same time.

There are two goals to aim for where squirrels and your sunflower seed feeder are concerned: keeping squirrels from getting to the feeder; and, if they do manage to reach it, keeping them from eating seed or chewing the feeder apart as they go after the seed.

Baffling the Squirrels

By far the best way to minimize squirrel damage at your sunflower feeder is to concentrate on the first goal, keeping the squirrels from reaching the feeder. To do this, you must take the following steps:

1. Hang your feeder at least 8 feet away from the nearest access, such as tree trunk or limb, and 5 to 6 feet off the ground. Even this may require some adjustment if you encounter a squirrel with exceptional jumping ability. If you have a plastic tubular feeder that has a seed-catching tray at-

tachment which the squirrels are using as a landing platform, remove the tray.
2. Use baffles — round or umbrella-shaped physical barriers that squirrels are unable to crawl over — on any wire that leads to the feeder. There are some excellent clear plastic baffles sold by bird feeder companies, and we highly recommend them. Some people choose to make their own out of sheet metal or other slippery materials, but remember that they must be big enough so that the squirrel cannot crawl over them. You may have to experiment to determine the right size. Some people also place empty spools of thread or other objects on the wire to prevent squirrels from getting a footing. We have found that baffles work best.
3. If you have a pole-mounted feeder, place baffles at least 4 feet up on the pole below the feeder. Remember to place the feeder far enough away from trees so a squirrel cannot jump to it.
4. Offer cracked corn on the ground away from the sunflower feeder to divert squirrels.

Preventing Squirrels from Eating or Chewing at Your Feeder

Squirrels will be unable to chew at your feeder if it is made from tough plastic, such as Lexan, and has a metal bottom and top, as well as metal-reinforced portals where the birds get the seed. See tips under "Choosing a Sunflower Feeder" in the chapter on sunflower feeders, p. 2.

In addition, there are several types of feeders that actually prevent squirrels from eating out of them once they land on them. One design is a plastic tubular feeder surrounded by a grid of tough, vinyl-coated wire. Another is made of steel and has a platform on which the weight of a squirrel, but not lighter birds, closes the feeder door.

UNDERSTANDING SQUIRRELS

Gray Squirrels

In summer, you will notice that gray squirrels are most active at your feeders in the early morning and then again in midafternoon; during the middle of the day they rest. In the winter, when the days are shorter, their peak activity is at noontime. When not active, gray squirrels often stay in their nest, an 18-inch-round accumulation of leaves and twigs placed near the top of a tree. Some people mistake these for birds' nests. Look for squirrels carrying bunches of leaves in their mouths and follow where they go; they are taking the leaves to their nest. Squirrels sleep in the nest and raise their young there.

Gray squirrels live in home ranges of several acres that overlap the home ranges of other gray squirrels. They do not defend these. However, gray squirrels establish a dominance hierarchy with other squirrels they meet. Watch the squirrels in your yard to see which are dominant. In general, older male squirrels are dominant over females and younger squirrels.

Like birds, squirrels use certain behaviors to communicate with one another. A dominant gray squirrel will chatter its teeth, stamp its feet, and wave its tail. It may run at and chase another squirrel, but actual fights are rare. When alarmed, squirrels also rapidly wave their tail forward and back.

Another type of chasing occurs during the breeding season, which is twice a year, in December to January and June to July. Female gray squirrels give off a special scent at this time that attracts males. Look for one squirrel being chased by a line of other squirrels. This will be a female followed by two or more males. The ones immediately behind her are the more dominant males, and one of them will probably be allowed to mate with her.

Watch squirrels as they move through the trees and you will notice that they tend to use the same connecting branches all the time. You may even see them pause and sniff a limb or rub their face on a limb. Squirrels leave scent marks and are able to tell from smelling these marks which other squirrels have been there.

To bury a nut, a gray squirrel digs a hole about 3 to 4 inches deep, puts the nut inside, pushes it down with its nose, and then pulls the earth over it with its front paws. How does the squirrel find the nut again? When it wants a winter meal, it goes to the general area and locates the nut either by the smell of the nut or its own scent, which was left when it helped bury the nut with its nose. Since more than one squirrel can bury nuts in the same area, it is not known who gets which nuts.

Red Squirrels

Red squirrels lead solitary lives, and each defends a territory of between 2 and 5 acres from other red squirrels, gray squirrels, and even some birds. Despite its smaller size, a red squirrel is much more feisty than a gray squirrel and will regularly chase the larger gray squirrel out of its territory. Red squirrels have two breeding seasons, March to May and July to September.

Unlike gray squirrels, red squirrels store most of their food in a central spot in their territory. This cache of nuts and cones may be in an underground chamber or under a brush pile. The squirrel will retrieve food and eat it above ground, often in the same spot. Look for telltale piles of discarded pinecone scales, which indicate a favorite eating spot.

Red squirrels live in leafy nests in trees or in underground tunnels that they dig.

A red squirrel having a snack.

TROUBLESHOOTING

THERE ARE NO BIRDS AT MY FEEDER

— Be sure that you have the kind of feeding setup that we have recommended. If you have the right feeders, seed, and plantings in your yard, be patient—the birds will arrive. In some areas it takes the birds longer to find and use feeders than in other areas.

— It may be the wrong season. At certain times of year—especially late summer, fall, and early winter—there is often an abundance of weed seeds and berries for birds to eat, so they do not need to come to your feeder. Also, in spring and early summer, birds have different social arrangements; they form pairs and are scattered over breeding territories. This is quite different than the situation in winter, when many of them remain in flocks and arrive at your feeder as a group. Even though you may see fewer birds in summer, you will get a special treat when they bring their babies to the feeder.

— It may be the wrong time of day. Many people say they have no birds and swear that they are watching their feeders all day. None of us watch feeders *all* day. Birds can come for very short periods to your feeder, such as right at daybreak, and then not come back at all; they may even come at dusk, when it is hard to see them. This frequently happens with cardinals. They may remain away from the feeder all day and show up only at dusk to feed. It may be too dark to see them, but you can tell when they arrive by listening for their "chip" call.

— Birds change their feeding behavior. Temperature, weather, time of year, time of day—all influence a bird's feeding habits. In mild weather, when wild food is plentiful, birds will use your feeder less. When they are under more pressure to find food, such as during snowstorms, they will come more regularly to your feeder.

— Some species come to feeders only in certain years. These include the pine siskin and evening grosbeak, which may be abundant one year and then absent the next, depending on how much food is available in the North. Many of the finches, such as goldfinches and purple finches, appear erratically at feeders and may wander widely in winter.

— Your neighbors may have put up feeders. And, heaven forbid, they may be more attractive than yours! Some birds may have gone to their feeders. If you follow our guidelines, you will maximize the attractiveness of your own feeders.

— You may live in a spot with very few birds. If there are not many trees, shrubs, or grasses in your area (be it urban or suburban), there will be no food or nesting areas and therefore few birds. Even with a good feeding station, you may not get birds. If you add trees and shrubs to your property, you may be surprised at how many more birds you will attract.

CATS OR HAWKS ARE EATING BIRDS AT MY FEEDER

What to Do About Cats

— Eliminate any possible hiding places around feeders so that birds can easily see cats in the area.

— Place birdbaths off the ground and away from shrubbery where cats could hide.

— Fence in ground feeders that are near brush piles or shrubbery.

What to Do About Hawks

There are several species of hawks that prey on small birds. The most common species are the sharp-shinned hawk in the East and Cooper's hawk in the West.

Hawks are protected by law. The best solution to dealing with their presence is to provide your songbirds with lots of places to seek shelter if a hawk appears. We have dense shrubbery and brush piles on our property, and our birds dive for cover when a hawk is in the area.

Other Concerns

Some people are concerned that birds' feet or eyes will freeze to the metal parts of bird feeders. Birds' feet do not have sweat glands, so they will not freeze to metal, and the reflexes of a healthy bird are so quick it is unlikely their eyes would touch metal.

A sharp-shinned hawk.

"UNDESIRABLE" BIRDS ARE AT MY FEEDER

Some people feel that certain birds are more desirable than others. We do not feel this way. We try to attract all the birds we can, for we love all birds, and each has fascinating behavior to observe and enjoy. Also, birds attract other birds, so a busy feeding station is highly desirable.

It is true that large birds can eat great quantities of seed, and that can be expensive. Also, some larger birds will beat out small birds for food. Our basic tactic is to offer something for everyone. Offer the expensive sunflower seed to the smaller birds in the kinds of hanging feeders designed for them. Offer the larger birds the less expensive cracked corn and mixed seed in ground feeders. There still may be times when you want to discourage certain birds. The best way to do this is to notice what they are eating and temporarily remove that food.

BIRDS KEEP CRASHING INTO OUR WINDOWS

Birds see the reflections of sky and trees in windows and mistake them for open space. This occurs especially when they are frightened and suddenly take wing or when they are new to the area, as when they are migrating. If this occurs often, there are several solutions. One is to eliminate the reflection of the windows by putting a screen up or taping newspaper outside them. Another solution is to buy or make a black silhouette of a diving sharp-shinned hawk or falcon and place it on the outside of your window.

Birds instinctively recognize that shape as meaning danger and will stay away from the window.

A silhouette of a merlin (hawk) on your window may keep birds from flying into it.

PLANTINGS THAT ATTRACT BIRDS

The most important concept in attracting birds is variety. Birds live in different habitats, and the greater the variety of habitats you create in your yard, the more birds you will attract.

A significant aspect of creating different habitats is offering food and nest sites at all levels. There are basically four levels you should try to create:
— Grass level, 2 inches to 1 foot high
— Shrub level, 2 to 5 feet high
— Small tree level, 5 to 15 feet high
— Tall tree level, 15 to 40 feet high

Try to add to your property whatever levels of vegetation are missing. Our property originally had only tall trees, so we have added lawn, shrubs, and small trees.

WHAT TO PLANT

From extensive experience in our yard and in the wild, we have come up with some simple criteria for choosing plants to attract birds. The best plants do two things:

1. *Produce berries or seeds that birds eat.* We try to choose the most prolific plants and also ones on which berries or seeds ripen at different seasons, so that food is offered all year.
2. *Provide places for nesting.* Although many shrubs and small trees produce food for birds, very few also have branching structures that are dense enough to support nests but not so dense that the birds cannot move among them easily.

A varied habitat attracts the most species of birds. This lovely yard offers lawn, hummingbird flowers, shrubs, small trees, tall trees, and lots of edge habitats.

Below are our recommendations for the best plants to buy that offer food *and* nesting support at each level. In some cases they are specific plants and their full scientific name is listed. In other cases they are a genus of plants from which you can choose any species that might be recommended by your local nurseryman.

Best Bird Plantings

Shrub level:
1. Honeysuckle, *Lonicera* spp.; get shrubs, not vines
2. Juniper, *Juniperus* spp.; get shrub species that grow 2 to 5 feet tall
3. Barberry, *Berberis* spp.

Small tree level:
1. Crab apple, *Malus* spp.; get species with abundant, small apples
2. Juniper, *Juniperus* spp.; get tree species that grow 10 to 20 feet tall
3. Hawthorn, *Crataegus* spp.

Tall tree level (try to offer a variety of foliage and foods):
1. Cones and cover: Pine, spruce, hemlock
2. Seeds: Maple, ash (female tree), elm, birch
3. Berries: Cherry, mulberry, mountain ash
4. Nuts: Oak

For more extensive listings of plantings for birds, see the publications listed in "Resources," p. 84.

SIX EASY WAYS TO CREATE A VARIETY OF HABITATS

— Create one or more loose piles of brush with limbs, branches, and old Christmas trees.
— Let part of your lawn grow tall and don't mow it. It should be a minimum of 10 feet by 10 feet.
— If there is a part of your yard that is overgrown with weeds and shrubs, leave it alone.
— Leave dead trees standing and dead limbs on trees, as long as they are not a hazard to anyone.
— If you are surrounded by trees, cut down enough to create a clearing.
— If you are surrounded by a clearing, plant a few shrubs and trees.

NEST BOXES

A good all-purpose nest box that is useful to almost all small hole-nesting birds but whose entrance hole is small enough to keep out the aggressive starling is detailed on the right. It can be placed 3 to 10 feet high on a tree or post just about anywhere on your property that is not often disturbed by human activity. For best results, it should be put up in fall or winter so the birds have a chance to get used to it. In addition to nesting in them, many birds — such as woodpeckers, swallows, and nuthatches — use the boxes for roosting in at night.

Be sure to drill holes along the tops of the sides for ventilation. Cedar is a good wood to use, and it does not need to be stained. If you use pine, you can preserve it with a coat of linseed oil.

Although endless variations of this basic box can be made, we find that this is the best all-purpose box. We have had chickadees, nuthatches, titmice, wrens, bluebirds, woodpeckers, and tree swallows nest in this type of box. Four or five of these boxes per acre is none too many. Place them in a variety of habitats and at different heights; experiment. Not all will be used every year, but by having several boxes you provide more choices for the birds.

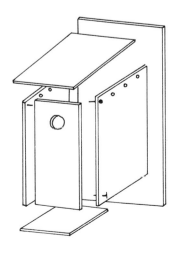

This is a good all-around bird box that will attract many of your favorite birds. The front can be hinged at the top with two nails so you can look in at the birds and clean out the box at the end of the season.
DIMENSIONS
Top: 8 × 7
Sides: 8 × 5 × 10
Front: 4½ × 8
Bottom: 4½ × 5
Back: 7 × 13
Hole: 1½ diameter

BIRD BEHAVIOR

WATCHING BIRD BEHAVIOR

One of the rewards of having birds at your feeders is a deeper sense of connection to nature, a constant reminder that there is more to life than only human concerns. The birds provide a balance and perspective to your view of life that will be even more pronounced if you take the time to watch birds and observe their behavior. As you begin to do this, you will find that you no longer think of them as little feathered creatures with human-given names, but instead as intricate, living things with their own language, social structures, and complex adaptations for survival.

Behavior-watching is one of the fastest-growing activities within bird-watching. It attracts people who are interested in a bird's whole life, who want to know the what, why, and how of each bird they see, and who generally find each species an endless source of discovery.

The goal of behavior-watching is to gain a deeper understanding of any bird you happen to encounter. It takes very little time, is easy to do, and is extremely rewarding; all it requires is focusing on an individual bird and watching what it does. Your watching may be as brief as fifteen seconds or as long as five to ten minutes. In either case we guarantee that if you look closely, you will see something new every time you look. We have been looking at our feeder birds for years, and we continue to discover new things all the time.

The Importance of Questions

Besides your eyes and ears, the most important thing to bring to your observing is your curiosity. Questions are the driving force behind all learning, and the more you ask, the more you will learn from what you see.

In most cases we have found that when it comes to questions, the simpler the better. Also, don't worry too much about not having all the answers — just continue to ask and be open to learning. It was once said that an expert is someone who is afraid to learn something new; in other words, it is better to be a good explorer than someone who believes they have all the answers. There is always more to learn.

Many of your questions about feeder birds will be answered in the individual chapters on each bird later on in the book, but some others may never have been answered, even by scientists and researchers. This is because there are very few people who take the time to observe nature as you will at your feeder. This may sound amazing, but it is true. There are many kinds of scientific discoveries that could be made right at your feeder but have not, simply because people have not taken the time.

On the next page are some questions you should try to answer as you watch your feeder birds; they will help you get started behavior-watching and exploring the lives of your feeder birds.

Questions About Feeding

Do they feed in flocks or alone? Do they feed on the ground and/or above ground? Do they take one seed at a time and then leave to eat it, or stay and continuously feed at the feeder? Do they prefer certain foods?

Questions About Interactions

How does the bird react to others at the feeder? Is it aggressive toward other birds, or is it tolerant? Does it make sounds or gestures at other birds while feeding? Does one member of a flock seem to be dominant over the others? Does one species seem to be dominant over other species?

Here a male red-winged blackbird is performing a territorial display.

TWO EASY WAYS TO BE A BETTER BEHAVIOR-WATCHER

As you begin to watch birds, ask questions, and get answers through this guide, we have two important tips. They have to do with making assumptions about what you see. If you can avoid making these two assumptions, you will be a much better behavior-watcher.

The "Little Feathered People" Assumption

Do not assume that birds are like people or that they have motives and emotions like ours. Instead, just watch what they actually do and see how they do it.

For example, a blue jay at your ground feeder may pick up a seed, hop over to another blue jay that is fluttering its wings, and feed it the seed.

Some people might describe this scene by saying that a mother jay fed a seed to a young jay which was begging. But this description makes several assumptions: that the action took place between a parent and young bird; that the young bird was begging; and that the adult was the mother.

In fact, you cannot be sure of any of these conclusions with blue jays. You cannot tell male from female by appearance; the bird that was fed may have been demanding food rather than begging; and after a few weeks out of the nest, young blue jays look like the adults. It is true that the behavior of a parent blue jay and its young as the parent feeds it is extremely similar to this, but so is blue jay courtship, in which the male feeds the female.

Therefore, by making assumptions about birds — assumptions that are in part based on human interactions — we may misinterpret bird behavior; this keeps us from seeing what birds are *really* like.

The "He-She" Assumption

One of the most frequent assumptions made by observers, as shown in the previous example, is that a bird is male or female before they really know which sex it is. People either unthinkingly call all birds "he," since this is common usage, or they assume it is a he or a she based on its behavior and the stereotypes we have about the roles of the sexes.

Either of these practices can be very limiting to your observations. If, when behavior-watching, you call all birds "he," you are simply wrong 50 percent of the time, and if you call them "he" or "she" based on your assumptions, you are missing the chance to see birds as they really are.

An easy solution is to call all birds "it" until you are sure about whether they are male or female. In addition, look at the sections on each bird and learn in which species male and female look alike and in which they look different.

SOCIAL BEHAVIOR

Bird behavior at your feeder can be divided into two types: social behavior and maintenance behavior. Social behavior is any interaction between birds (i.e., aggression, courtship, flocking, breeding), whereas maintenance behavior includes all that a bird does to maintain itself (preening, bathing, eating, sleeping). Below are some common social behaviors that you will see while birds are at your feeder; descriptions of maintenance behaviors follow on p. 22.

Interactions

Whenever two or more birds are at a feeder, there are interactions. They can be fascinating and can provide endless hours of entertainment.

Most interactions at feeders are aggressive. This is because you have provided a rich, unending source of food in a limited space, causing birds to compete for the food. The more feeders you have and the more spread out they are, the less competition and aggression there will be.

Many feeder birds — such as chickadees, sparrows, goldfinches, blue jays, and pine siskins — feed in flocks during winter. Because of this, they are often competing with other members of their flock for food. Instead of fighting with each other all the time, which takes extra energy and involves the risk of injury, the birds in these flocks form a hierarchy in which they recognize each other and, in a sense, have agreed upon who gets food first. When two birds in the flock show up at the same spot, the more dominant one will be allowed to feed first, and the other will leave or wait without challenging it. A bird's placement in the hierarchy may be determined by one or more factors, such as its sex, age, plumage, or individual level of aggression.

When observing interactions between birds at your feeder, try to answer some of these questions: Who initiates the interaction? What happens during it? What is the result of the interaction? Is it between the same or different species? You may want to record the answers in your bird feeder journal and build up your own library of facts about each species.

Language

Birds communicate with each other through gestures and sounds. These gestures and sounds are called displays, and each species has a fixed set of displays that makes up its "language." Many of the displays given at feeders communicate dominance or subordinance between members of a flock.

All bird sounds have evolved for communication, and each different sound of a given bird probably has a different function. Do not expect to get an exact meaning, in words, of a call, for bird sounds are not like sentences or words — they are more like expressions of an emotional state. For the meanings of these sounds, read *A Guide to Bird Behavior*, volumes I and II, by Donald and Lillian Stokes.

Each species also has its own special gestures, which are a part of its language. These generally are unusual postures of the feathers or body. Three common visual displays used by many feeder birds are described below.

Head Forward: The bird is horizontal with its bill pointing at another bird. Sometimes its bill is "gaped" (open). This gesture is often done by a goldfinch or siskin that is perched at the feeder and being challenged for its spot by another bird.

Crest Raise: The feathers on the top of the bird's head are raised. Given not only by birds with obvious crests, such as titmice and cardinals, but also by chickadees, goldfinches, woodpeckers, and sparrows, the display is brief, sometimes lasting only a second. It is often done by a bird that has just landed at a feeder and is trying to find a space to feed.

Wing Droop: The bird's tail is slightly raised and its wingtips lowered, making them look like points below the tail. This display may be held for several seconds and signals aggression or dominance.

Another sign of dominance is one bird flying at another and displacing it from its perch or spot. This is called displacement or perch-taking and is common at feeders. The bird that does the displacing is the dominant one.

Alarm Behavior

Birds have two types of predators: Those that approach on the ground, such as a human, a cat, or a snake; and those that approach from the air, such as a hawk. They respond to each of these in a different way.

When there is a ground predator, the birds usually fly up to perches nearby and start to make short harsh calls like "check, check" or "chip, chip." They keep the predator in view and usually keep calling until it leaves.

With an aerial predator, usually the bird that first sees it gives a very high-pitched whistle, causing all other birds in the area to immediately become silent and freeze. You can see this at your feeder. When the birds are quiet and absolutely still, with only their eyes looking actively in all directions, this probably means there is a sharp-shinned hawk or Cooper's hawk in the vicinity, for these are the main aerial predators at feeders. The feeder birds may remain frozen in this manner for several minutes before resuming normal activity. We often have been made aware of these hawks simply through the behavior of our feeder birds.

Social Arrangements

In spring and summer, most birds stay in pairs as they go about the various stages of breeding. But in fall and winter, these pairs often break up, and the birds form different social groupings. Below is a list of some of these arrangements and the birds that are most commonly found in them.

Lone Birds: Some birds, after breeding, remain as lone individuals throughout winter, usually on a fixed range or territory. Examples: mockingbird, towhee, cardinal (occasionally), song sparrow (occasionally).

Pairs: A few of our feeder birds remain together as mated pairs on their breeding territory throughout the year. Examples: nuthatches, woodpeckers, mockingbirds (occasionally), cardinals (occasionally).

Many of the interactions at feeders are aggressive, such as the head-forward threat of this male American goldfinch.

Family Group: In some species the young stay with the parents through the first winter. This is the case with the tufted titmouse, the crow, and possibly the blue jay.

Small Flock: Some birds that winter as small flocks may be in family groups; others may not. Birds that form flocks include chickadees, titmice, cardinals, towhees, sparrows, cowbirds, house sparrows, and finches.

Large Flock: Many feeder birds stay in large flocks during winter, often roaming widely as a flock. Examples: goldfinches, mourning doves, pigeons, starlings, sparrows, juncos, red-winged blackbirds, common grackles, house sparrows, pine siskins, evening grosbeaks.

Mixed Flock: Sometimes flocks are composed of more than one species, possibly because several species can benefit from traveling in larger groups, gaining protection from predators and knowledge of new feeding areas. Examples of mixed flocks include chickadee-titmouse-nuthatch-woodpecker; junco–tree sparrow; siskin-goldfinch.

MAINTENANCE BEHAVIOR

Maintenance behavior comprises all the actions a bird does to maintain itself. It differs from social behavior in that it generally does not involve interacting with another bird. Below are the most common maintenance behaviors that you may see at or around your feeder.

Feeding

Every bird feeds in a slightly different manner, and it can be a lot of fun to watch and discover all of the various methods. For example, you have probably noticed that chickadees, titmice, and nuthatches most often take one seed from the feeder and then go to another perch to eat it, while birds like grosbeaks, goldfinches, siskins, and mourning doves may stay in one spot and keep eating seed after seed.

Some birds typically come to ground feeders, others to hanging feeders. This usually reflects what they most commonly eat in the wild. For instance, mourning doves feed on fallen weed seeds and will always come to your ground feeder, while goldfinches feed on tree and weed seeds and will come to your hanging feeder. Birds such as woodpeckers and chickadees, which feed on many insects found in tree bark, are more comfortable coming to feeders that are high off the ground, like the suet and hanging sunflower feeder. Some birds, including blue jays and starlings, feed on a variety of foods at any level where they can find them and so may be seen at any of your feeders.

A few of our feeder birds have the habit of taking seeds and nuts and storing them for later use. Nuthatches often make repeated trips when they are storing food, and it is easy to spot them leaving the feeder, landing on a nearby tree trunk, and stuffing the seed into a bark crevice. Blue jays store acorns under the ground, and this helps replant forests.

Drinking and Bathing

If you supply water near your feeders, you will see birds coming to drink and bathe. To drink, most birds collect a small bit of water in their bill and then tilt their head back to let the water run into their throat. This tilting is necessary because they cannot suck water up through their bill. The exception is members of the dove family, including the pigeon and mourning dove. These birds can suck up water and thus continually sip without tilting their head back.

Many birds get water in winter by pecking at ice or eating snow. We once saw a flock of cedar waxwings repeatedly flying out and back from their perches in a tree as if they were catching insects. But is was a cold winter day and snowing, and as we looked more closely through our binoculars we saw that they were catching snowflakes in midair.

Bathing behavior varies from species to species. Many birds stand in shallow water and, through a complex series of movements — rolling their head and body and fluttering their wings — get water trapped in featherless areas next to their body and then press the water out through their feathers. Some aerial birds, like swallows, may dive into water and immediately fly up. Still others may jump into water and be briefly submerged before getting out. Some birds bathe in rain or drizzle, in dew on grass, or among wet leaves. Take time to watch bathing behavior; it is fascinating.

Sunbathing

On a sunny day you may see a bird adopt a strange pose, its wings spread out and body feathers fluffed. If it remains in this pose for a minute or more, chances are that the bird is sunbathing. Scientists are still studying why birds sunbathe. Two theories are that the rays of the sun help the bird produce vitamin D or that sunlight is soothing to a bird's skin during molting. Birds usually sunbathe while lying on the ground in an open area, and while doing it they often look as if they are in a trance.

Molting

Birds lose and regrow their feathers once or twice a year. This is called molting, and it can be observed at your feeder, where you can get a close look. All of our feeder birds have a complete molt of all their feathers in late summer and early fall, gradually losing and regrowing their feathers in a fixed sequence. The birds start to look unkempt and rather ragged at this time, and there are often blotches of different colors as new feathers grow in. They may also be missing certain tail or wing feathers. Birds that have finished molting have a perfect set of feathers, which are particularly beautiful. Look for evidence of this molt in August and September.

Some of our feeder birds have another molt in the spring, but this involves only their body feathers and not their wings and tail. Look for this in March through May. A bird that goes through a spring molt is the American goldfinch. In winter, the male and female look similar and are more of a gray-yellow than in summer. After they molt in the spring, the female is more yellow, and the male is bright yellow with a black patch on his forehead.

Each bird species has different sources of food. This cedar waxwing is feeding on berries of the highbush cranberry.

A YEAR IN THE LIFE OF A BIRD

All birds have a yearly cycle of behavior. Being familiar with this cycle will enable you to place the behavior you see at your feeder in the larger context of a bird's whole life. Because this makes bird behavior at your feeder more meaningful and enjoyable, we have included here a short summary of a year in the life of a typical bird. Clearly this is a generalized account, for each bird is slightly different.

Start of Breeding / Migration

The breeding season for most small birds starts in late winter or spring when the changing lengths of daylight (photoperiod) trigger hormonal changes in the birds, which in turn result in changed behavior. For birds that migrate, such as red-winged blackbirds, the photoperiod may cause their migration north to their breeding ground. Other birds that are year-round residents of an area, such as white-breasted nuthatches, may begin to restrict their movements to a nesting area.

Territory Formation

The beautiful singing of birds in spring is one of the supreme delights of nature. Most singing is done by males, and it generally has two functions: to advertise and defend a territory against other males, and to attract a female to the territory. If other males of the same species try to intrude on the territory, then there are bouts of displaying, chases, or occasional direct fighting. Once territories are agreed upon among birds and a bird has a mate, singing is much reduced or stops completely.

Courtship

The magical behavior we tend to lump under the simple name of courtship is far from understood in any animal (and probably least of all in our own species). It involves close interactions and displays between males and females, which result in a kind of bonding or mutual benefit that keeps a pair of animals together. In migratory birds, females usually arrive slightly after males have established territories, soon after which males and females begin to "court"—choose mates and form pairs. Once paired, the male and female are much more synchronized in their activities and tend to stay together as they move about the territory.

Nest-Building

Nest-building usually starts soon after courtship is completed. In most species, all building is done by the female, with the male often following her to and from the nest as she gathers materials. The male may build the foundation and the female add the lining in some species, such as the house wren. In other species, like cedar waxwings, both sexes participate. Nest-building normally takes from a few days to about a week to complete.

Mating and Egg-Laying

To mate, the male steps onto the back of the female and bends his tail down as she lifts hers up. The anal openings, or cloaca, of the male and female touch, and sperm is transferred. After a few seconds the male steps off the female's back.

The female lays one egg per day, usually early each morning. Four to six eggs is a common number for most small species. The birds generally do not spend very much time at the nest until most of the eggs are laid.

Incubation

Incubation does not usually start until the day before the last egg is laid, probably so that all the eggs will hatch on the same day. In most species, only the female incubates. She actually develops added blood vessels on her breast and may lose some of her feathers at the same spot. This area, called the brood patch, is like a little heating pad that warms the eggs. During this period the male may bring food to the female, or he may guard the nest while the female takes breaks and feeds. Incubation lasts about ten to twelve days in small birds.

Nestling Phase

Once the eggs have hatched, things get really busy at the nest, for the young call from the nest and the parents have to make repeated trips with food. The young are called nestlings because they remain in the nest and are fed by the parents. For the first few days of the nestling phase the young birds need to be "brooded" — have an adult sit over them — since they have no feathers and cannot keep warm. Soon they develop feathers and no longer need to be brooded. The nestling phase lasts about ten days.

Fledgling Phase

After the young leave the nest they are called fledglings. Although they are out of the nest, they are still dependent on the parents for food. Fledglings often sit and call continuously, and the adults may feed them less frequently than when they were nestlings but with larger pieces of food. Gradually, the fledglings will begin to find food on their own. This phase may end abruptly with the parents becoming ag-

gressive to their young and chasing them away. The fledgling phase lasts from one to several weeks.

Migration

The fall migration of birds is always exciting. Bird populations are greatest just before migration because there are many new young birds from the summer's breeding. Migration usually starts after the birds have completed their molt. Birds that do not migrate will remain in the same area that they bred in or will move to nearby areas with better food.

In winter, most pairs are less closely associated with each other. This continues until the following breeding season. For more on social arrangements in winter, see the chapter "Social Behavior," p. 20.

Life Span of Birds

The most difficult time for a bird to live through is the first year of its life, for it has so much to learn. If it lives for one year, it has a good chance of living for several more. Even so, the average life span for most small birds, such as those at your feeder, is about two to five years. Larger birds, such as crows, may live ten years or more.

This is the nestling phase of cardinal breeding, during which the parents bring food to the young in the nest.

FOUR BEHAVIORS EVERYONE ASKS ABOUT

Through the years we have had a chance to hear thousands of people tell us about bird behavior they have seen. Since some questions about behavior repeatedly crop up, we have given answers to four of the most common.

Why is this bird pecking on my window?

Many people have had cardinals, robins, titmice, and other species pecking at their windows or car mirrors, often at the same spot, day after day. This window-pecking usually occurs in spring and summer.

Explanation: The bird sees the reflection of what it believes is another bird of the same species and sex in the glass and responds aggressively to it. It usually occurs during the breeding season, since that is when birds are defending mates and territories. If you cover up the reflection, the birds will stop pecking.

Why are woodpeckers drumming on my house?

Homeowners often complain of woodpeckers doing long, rapid series of drumming on the side of their house, gutter, drainpipe, or even TV antenna. They are disturbed by the noise, afraid the bird will demolish their home, and concerned about whether they have bugs in the house that the bird is going after.

Explanation: When woodpeckers go after insects, they tap in an irregular rhythm, generally not very loud, to open a hole in the wood. If this is the case, then look where the woodpecker is pecking and check for insect activity.

If the woodpecker's taps are loud, rapid volleys, then the woodpecker is "drumming." Drumming in woodpeckers is like song in other birds — it announces the bird's territory and may attract a mate. It is also a way in which the male and female keep in touch. The birds pick resonant spots to drum on and then continue to use them through the beginning of the breeding season. No wood will be excavated and no damage done to your house, although you may be woken up early in the morning. The drumming will stop once the breeding season is under way. You can put cloth or something else over the drumming spot to make it less resonant.

Why do mockingbirds repeatedly raise and lower their wings in a stiff, mechanical way?

This is often seen as the birds are on the ground.

Explanation: This is called wing-flashing. Although nobody is really sure why the birds do it, there are two theories about its function. It may cause insects to move and make them more obvious to the feeding bird, for when it is given by a lone mockingbird on the ground, the bird usually is looking for food. The other theory is that wing-flashing is aggressive, often being directed at other mockingbirds and occasionally preceding an attack. We have seen this display in fall when many young mockingbirds were traveling through areas already occupied by adult mockingbirds.

Why do birds pick up ants or other materials and rub their feathers with them?

In this behavior, which is striking but not often seen, birds may sit on an ant nest or take cigarette butts or mothballs and use them to rub their feathers.

Explanation: These actions represent a complex behavior generally termed "anting" because it most often occurs with ants. It is believed somehow to maintain the feathers and/or skin of the bird. Chemicals from the ants or other materials may help rid the bird of feather parasites, a common problem, or soothe the skin as new feathers grow in.

Woodpeckers often drum on houses to signal to each other. This is a female red-bellied woodpecker.

THE BIRDS

IDENTIFYING YOUR BIRDS

This book has been designed to help you identify your feeder birds. We have included all the species that are common at feeders over a significant portion of the country. Under each species's behavioral description is a photograph of the bird with the most important identifying clues noted in the caption beneath. In cases where the male and female of a species look different from each other, there is a photograph of each with identifying clues. For each species, a range map describes the winter range (indicated by diagonal lines on a white background) and the summer range (indicated by shading). The areas marked by diagonal lines on a dark background are where the bird lives year-round.

Bird identification involves looking and listening. It is a skill that anybody can learn, and you will get better with practice. You may want binoculars if your feeders are away from the house; in fact, we use them whether the birds are near or far, for it is exciting to see their beauty in such detail.

HOW TO LOOK AT A BIRD

The first thing to do when identifying a bird is look at its body:
1. Notice its size. Is it small like a sparrow? Medium-sized like a robin? Or large like a crow?
2. Look at the colors on its breast, wings, and tail. Is the bird a uniform color? Are there any conspicuous patches of color on the wings or tail? Is there streaking or different colors on the breast?

Then look at its head:
1. Look at the shape and colors of the head. Is it all one color? Is it iridescent? Does it have a stripe through the eye? Is the shape of the head distinctive? Does the bird have a crest?

2. Look at the shape and color of the bill. Is it long or short? Conical or thin? Is it all one color?

The most common mistake beginners make is not getting enough clues while the bird is in sight. Instead, they run to their identification guide, find they do not remember the bird well enough to locate it in the guide, and then look back for the bird, by which time it is gone.

Therefore, when you first see a bird, take time to watch it and pick up as many clues as you can. Try to remember them, repeating them to yourself as you watch the bird. Then go to this book for identification.

Another aid in bird identification is the process of elimination. Deciding what a bird is *not* will help narrow down your choices of what it *is*.

Look at the photographs of the birds in this guide during a leisure moment and read the identification clues beneath them. This will familiarize you with the various species and help you identify them when they are at your feeder. Become familiar with all the common birds, for then you will be more alert to any unusual birds that show up.

Finally, once you have identified a bird, continue to add to your list of ways to identify it — see where it feeds, how it flies, how it interacts with other birds, and listen for the sounds it makes. All of these things will help you identify it more easily in the future.

A WORD ABOUT BINOCULARS

When buying binoculars, the birder is faced with a large variety from which to choose. Here are a few guidelines.

There are two sets of numbers on a pair of binoculars that you need to pay attention to. One of these, usually found near the eyepieces, will read something like *7.5 × 35*. The first of these figures — 7.5 — is the power of the magnification; for good bird-watching, this should be between 7.5 and 8.5. The second figure — 35 — is the diameter of the largest lens and indicates how much light is let in, which will affect how well you see the image. Anywhere from 35 to 50 is good for birding.

The second set of numbers, also near the eyepieces, expresses how wide-angle the binoculars are. If the numbers read *430 ft / 1,000 yds*, at 1,000 yards you will have a field of vision 430 feet wide. Sometimes this is expressed as the number of degrees of a circle that you can see at 1,000 yards; for example, 7 degrees. Binoculars that are over 7 degrees, or more than 350 feet at 1,000 yards, are good.

The binoculars you buy should also have a central focusing knob and be light enough for you to hold comfortably. Some good companies that make reliable binoculars are Swift and Bushnell.

CARDINAL

Northern Cardinal / *Cardinalis cardinalis*

How the Cardinal Got Its Name

The word *cardinal* originally meant "important" and later referred to the high-ranking official in the Roman Catholic Church. After that it became associated with the bright red color of the cardinal's robes, and through this chain of events finally became the name of the bird.

How to Attract Cardinals

If you have the right habitat in your yard, you should be able to attract cardinals. They like to live in generally open areas that have both trees and berry-producing shrubs. They usually build their nests in dense thickets or low shrubs or vines that lie an average of 4 to 5 feet off the ground. Cardinals also sleep in these dense tangles. Some of their favorite plants include honeysuckle, evergreens, privet, and multiflora rose.

Cardinals prefer those feeding stations that offer seed on a tray, platform, or just scattered on the ground. Although they relish sunflower seed, they do eat a variety of other foods, including cracked corn, millet, safflower seed, and nutmeats. When eating sunflower, they manipulate the seed with their tongue until it lies sideways in their powerful bill, crack it open, eject the hull with their tongue, and swallow the seed.

A Beautiful Duet

We were awakened one early spring morning by the most beautiful singing coming from our yard. As we listened, we realized it sounded like a duet, with one bird singing a certain series of phrases and another bird repeating those phrases exactly. It sounded a little like this: "Whoit, whoit, whoit . . . whoit, whoit, whoit . . . what-cheer, what-cheer, what-cheer . . . what-cheer, what-cheer, what-cheer."

We knew it was the cardinals in our yard, but since both male and female cardinals can sing, we

Northern cardinal, adult female. A medium-sized bird with a crest, olive-to-buffy-brown body, reddish wings and tail, and a bright red bill.

Northern cardinal, fledgling. It is similar to the adult female but has a gray-to-black bill instead of a red one, as in the adult.

Northern cardinal, adult male. A medium-sized, all-red bird with a crest and an area of black surrounding its red bill.

Northern cardinal range map

did not know whether this was the duet of a mated pair or of birds of the same sex. When done between male and female, it is part of courtship activities and strengthens the bonds between the pair. When given between cardinals of the same sex, it can mean each is defending its own territory.

Cardinals in different areas of the country may use different phrases in their songs. This is why cardinals in Missouri might sound different from cardinals in Ontario. Young cardinals learn their songs from adults in the area in which they live. And since cardinals rarely travel very great distances from where they were born, it's easy to see why birds in the same area would sound alike.

Flocks, Pairs, or Alone?

During the breeding season — midspring through summer — you will have either pairs or lone birds visit your feeder. But in winter, cardinals often join flocks in areas of abundant food and stay together until breeding starts. The flocks contain both males and females and reach sizes of fifty or more birds. In northern areas, where the cardinal has just recently moved in, winter flocks are less likely to occur, since the overall population of cardinals is still low.

Courtship Feeding

Through most of the winter, males are usually dominant over females at the feeder. Then a change occurs, and a lovely ceremony starts to take place in late winter and continues on through midsummer. You will see the male pick up a bit of food, go over to the female, and place it in her bill. This is called courtship feeding, or mate-feeding, and is a good sign that the birds are paired and about to start their breeding season.

Bird Feeder Journal

May 20, 9 A.M. The cardinals are nesting in the catbrier, very close to where cardinals nested two years ago. She is incubating four eggs. He takes sunflower seed from the feeder, flies near her, and sings softly. She comes off the nest, and he feeds her.

CHICKADEES

Black-Capped Chickadee / *Parus atricapillus*

Carolina Chickadee / *Parus carolinensis*

America's Favorite Feeder Bird

The chickadee is one of America's favorite feeder birds. On the dreariest winter days we are cheered up by watching them at our feeder.

Chickadees are remarkable because they have one of the most complex social structures of any feeder bird; they also have one of the largest "vocabularies" of calls. These two may be related — they may need a greater range of communication to keep the order in their complex flock structure.

Dictionary of Chickadee Calls

Chickadees make more than fifteen different sounds, but these are their most common.

"Chickadeedeedee" — Often given at disturbances or when one bird becomes separated from the rest of the flock. Given all year.

"Tseet" — A short, high, soft call given between members of a pair or a flock to help them keep in contact. Given all year.

"Feebee" — The song of the black-capped chickadee; a two-note whistle, with the second note lower than the first. The Carolina chickadee song is four notes that sound like "feebee feebay." Given by males to advertise territory and attract mates.

Carolina or Black-Capped?

From the range maps you can see that there are areas, especially in the mid-Atlantic states, where both the Carolina and black-capped chickadees live. If you live in one of these areas, you may want to distinguish between the two species. Everybody agrees that the males' songs differ markedly in the two species, and this is the best clue.

Distinguishing the two species by sight is difficult. When the two birds are together, the black-capped is slightly larger, has a longer tail, and has more white on the edge of its wing feathers.

Counting Chickadee Flocks

From March to August, chickadees live in pairs on territories of about 10 acres. But in August, when they are finished breeding, they start to gather into small flocks of about six to ten birds. These flocks are composed of adults who have bred in the area and young birds from other areas.

Each flock stays within and defends a territory of about 20 acres and chases out other chickadee flocks that enter. Thus, if your feeder is in a chickadee territory, you will have the same birds feeding there from August to March. Sometimes a feeder is near the border of two chickadee flock territories. When both flocks show up at once, you will see many chases and hear scolding calls.

Black-capped chickadee. A small bird with a black cap, black throat, and white cheek. The male and female look alike.

Black-capped chickadee range map

Different flocks often contain different numbers of birds. By counting the number of birds in a given flock you may be able to discover how many flocks you have. The best way to count the number of birds in a flock is to wait until they cross an open space, for they tend to cross one at a time.

In spring, the most dominant pairs of the flock breed in the area of the winter territory; the others are forced out and try to breed elsewhere.

Chickadee Courtship

At some point you are likely to see a chickadee near the feeder suddenly begin to quiver its wings, lean forward, and give a special call that sounds like "teeship teeship." In the spring this is done by the adult female, and in response her mate brings food to her and places it in her beak. In mid- to late summer this same wing-quivering and calling is done by fledglings as they beg for food from their parents. Some researchers prefer to call this demand behavior, since the female may be dominant over the male when she is being fed and young birds may in some sense be dominant over their parents when they are fledglings.

Watching Chickadees Feed

It is interesting that chickadees tend to take one seed from a feeder, fly away to a nearby perch and eat it, and then fly back for another. The seed is usually carried away in their bill and then held in their foot as they peck at it. In the wild they feed on tiny seeds and insects.

Chickadees visit the feeder one at a time while other chickadees wait nearby. This is because each flock has a fairly stable hierarchy throughout winter, and in general the most dominant bird is allowed to feed first. A dominant bird may also fly to the feeder and displace a less dominant bird.

Chickadees have amazing acrobatic abilities, enabling them to hang on upside down under the most delicate twigs. This adaptation allows them to feed on insects on the tips of branches and also to find insects on the underside of branches when the tops are covered with snow.

Ragged-Looking Chickadees

In late summer you may see fairly ragged-looking chickadees at your feeder. These are adults that are molting and whose feathers are particularly worn from repeatedly going in and out of their nest hole to

A black-capped chickadee inspecting a tree hole that could be a nest site.

Carolina chickadee range map

feed their young. On the other hand, you are also likely to see well-feathered, neat birds with clear white breasts at the feeder about the same time. These are usually young birds just born this season, and they are already adult size.

Bird Feeder Journal

April 30, 10:30 A.M. We have been watching a pair of chickadees excavate a nest hole in the top of a 2-foot-high rotting gray birch stub in our woods. Earlier this morning, as our son was clearing some brush, he accidentally dragged the brush over the stub, and it fell over. We decided to tie it together with string and stake it up. The chickadees called excitedly as we did this, but within minutes of our having resurrected the stub, the pair resumed their excavation as if nothing had happened! They successfully raised a brood from this nest.

COWBIRD

Brown-Headed Cowbird / *Molothrus ater*

The Buffalo Bird

Before people started clearing the forests of the eastern and western United States, the cowbird's range followed closely that of the buffalo herds, which roamed the Great Plains. The birds are believed to have followed the herds through summer, eating insects that the buffalo stirred up with their movements and ticks and other parasites off the animals' backs. They may also have followed herds of antelope throughout the same region.

Several things may have affected the cowbird's range. One was the fencing off of large areas of the West, restricting the movement of wild herds. Another was the introduction of cattle, from which the cowbird could obtain food in the same way it did from the wild herds. And finally, the clearing of land to the east and the addition of cows and cattle there probably enabled the cowbird to extend its range from coast to coast.

Distinguishing Male, Female, and Juvenile

The male and female look quite different. The male has a brown head, but the rest of his body, wings, and tail is black with a greenish, glossy iridescence. The female has fairly uniform gray-brown plumage with slightly darker wings and tail. The juvenile cowbird is similar in appearance to the female but has a brown-streaked breast.

The cowbirds belong to the family *Icteridae*, which includes blackbirds, orioles, and meadowlarks. Their body shape is similar to that of these cousins, but their bills are noticeably shorter and more conical.

Behavior at Your Feeder

The next time a small group of cowbirds visits your ground feeder, take a moment to watch them and you will most likely see some examples of cowbird language. Generally each bird maintains a distance from the others, but if one bird is approached too closely, it will fluff out its feathers, raise its wings, and thrust its head toward the intruding bird. This makes the other bird back away. If there is a stand-off, then both birds may briefly point their bills up in the air as another way of settling the disputed area. In some way this display — known as bill tilt — seems to communicate who is the dominant bird, and the other moves slightly away.

If you see a group of males and a female at your feeder, watch for cowbird courtship. A group of males usually competes among itself for dominance, and the winner gets the female. To compete, they use the bill tilt and another interesting gesture called topple-over, in which a male cowbird fluffs its body feathers, arches its neck, spreads its wings and tail, and seems to fall forward while giving its song, which sounds like "bublocomseee." The bird may then vigorously wipe its bill back and forth on the ground or on a perch. Courtship behavior begins when the birds arrive in spring and lasts until mid-June.

Problems of Being a Nest Parasite

The brown-headed cowbird makes no nest of its own; rather, it lays its eggs in other birds' nests and lets the other parents raise its young. Thus it is called a parasite. This seems like a pretty good arrangement for the cowbird, and you might wonder why more species do not do this and why we are not overrun with cowbirds.

The reason is that it is not as easy as it seems. First of all, the female cowbird must find other birds' nests just when the other birds are laying eggs, for she then removes one from the nest and lays her own there. Like other birds, she lays one egg a day and, therefore, must find four to five nests all ready at that time so she can deposit her eggs in them. The next problem is that many other birds can recognize a cowbird egg when it is laid in their nest, and they either take it out, abandon the nest, or build a new nest on top of it. Hence, cowbirds have a very low

Brown-headed cowbird, male and female. A medium-sized dark bird. The male has a brown head and black body with iridescence; the female is uniformly gray with no markings.

Brown-headed cowbird range map

success rate for their eggs — it has been estimated that a female cowbird lays about forty eggs per season with only two or three young surviving to adulthood.

This habit of laying eggs in other birds' nests may be a result of the cowbird's background of following the buffalo herds and not having time in any one place to build its own nest and raise young.

What Happens to a Baby Cowbird?

If a cowbird egg is laid in a nest and the host parent does not notice it, then the baby cowbird is on its way. It usually hatches slightly earlier than the other eggs, and it grows very fast in its first few days. These two adaptations give it an advantage over its nest mates, for it is larger and able to get more of the food the parents bring to the nest; this may slow the development of the original young. In many cases, a baby cowbird crowds one of the original young out of the nest, and it dies.

The parents feed the nestling cowbird as if it were one of their own, even though it is bigger and looks different from the other nestlings. The cowbird is usually the first to leave the nest and to be fed by the parents outside the nest. It is indeed a strange sight to see a yellow warbler adult feeding a fledgling cowbird that is twice its size. How a baby cowbird then proceeds to join its own species is still a mystery.

Cowbird Flocks

Cowbirds generally feed together in small or large flocks, depending on the season. In fall and spring, when they are in the process of migrating, they feed in large flocks in fields or agricultural areas. Each night they go to large communal roosts that may contain thousands of birds of several species, such as red-winged blackbirds, common grackles, and rusty blackbirds. During summer they may still go to communal roosts, but these are usually smaller and composed of only several hundred birds.

Bird Feeder Journal

May 12, 3 P.M. Several male cowbirds have landed at the ground feeder and are displaying to each other. They are doing the bill-tilt display almost to the point of not getting time to feed. They have now flown up to the top of a nearby tree and are doing topple-over displays. It is almost comical, for they all look as if they are going to fall off the branches. Each bird ends its display by wiping its bill several times across the branch.

AMERICAN CROW

American Crow / *Corvus brachyrhynchos*

Watching Crows Feed

Crows are undoubtedly the most wary of feeder birds. They usually land in nearby trees and take a good look in all directions before landing at your ground feeder. Even while some crows are feeding, one or more may remain in the trees, possibly acting as a lookout. If your feeder does not have open space around it, the crows may not come at all.

Crows eat just about any kind of seed but especially cracked corn and sunflower seeds. In the wild they feed on seeds, insects, fruit, earthworms, carrion, and garbage.

Watching Crow Behavior

One of our favorite activities is watching the behavior of crows around our feeders. For most of the year, crows seem to live in small groups of about four to seven birds. Recent research suggests that these are parents and young from the previous year or years. Each of these groups may occasionally defend their area against other groups, especially in spring, when breeding begins. Some of the ways you will see crows be aggressive are chasing each other in the air and, in a group, flying high and circling above another group.

When the crows are on the ground, they may perform several other displays. One is cawing with an exaggerated bowing of the head and body and with the wings partially opened; another is wiping the bill back and forth across a branch; and a third is repeatedly flicking the wings and tail. All of these actions can occur in other contexts, but when they occur together, chances are the crow is expressing aggression toward another crow.

Crow Conventions

Every winter afternoon we see the crows in our area fly off in the same direction, and then return early the next morning. One winter we became so curious as to where they went that we got in our car and tried to follow them. It was not easy keeping them in view as we crisscrossed on country roads. After several miles we saw them join with other crows. From then on the flock got larger with each mile.

After 20 miles of driving we noticed that all the crows were heading toward a parking lot in a shopping center. We went to the area, got out of the car, and watched. We were amazed, for we saw thousands of crows streaming in from about three different directions. They gathered in the tops of trees; around sundown, all went into a group of pine trees covering about a half acre. This was their roost for the night, and amazingly, once they were settled, it was hard to see or hear a single bird.

This roosting is typical of crows all across the country. Look for it in fall and winter. The birds start in afternoon, fly along fixed routes, stop briefly at pre-roost sites, where they gather with other flocks, and then move on to the final roost. Communal roosts are usually located in some protected spot, such as a group of evergreens or dense trees. A roost can be in the city or the country, and crows may fly as far as 50 miles each day to join it.

The final roost can contain from a few hundred to a hundred thousand crows, with the larger roosts usually occurring more in the South. In the morning, the crows leave and go back to where they feed during the day.

Why roosts form is something still being investigated by scientists and bird watchers. Much more careful observation of their behavior near and at roosts is needed to answer this question. For a few theories on why roosts form, see the chapter on the European starling (p. 74).

Mobbing Hawks and Owls

One of the best ways to discover the presence of a hawk or owl in your area is to be aware of the behavior of crows. When you hear several crows giving harsh, drawn-out caws and see them repeatedly diving into the top of a tree, chances are there is a hawk or owl in the tree; crows typically harass, or "mob," these birds of prey whenever they find them. The mobbing may continue for five or ten minutes before the bird of prey flies off to a new spot. When it takes flight, the crows follow and dive at it in flight and continue to caw. After ten or fifteen minutes the crows usually stop, but they may come back later and repeat the mobbing.

Why crows do this is still not clear. It is true that some hawks and owls can catch and eat crows and that to some extent the mobbing may discourage a hawk or owl from settling in an area with crows. But in most cases, little damage is done, and the hawk or owl ignores the crows. Some researchers suggest that mobbing helps teach young crows who their possible predators are. Blue jays, which belong to the same family as crows, also mob birds of prey.

Secretive Nester

We once had some crows build a nest within 20 yards of our house, but we knew nothing about it until we heard the young nestlings calling for food. The crow is so secretive around its nest that it is difficult even to see it building the nest. Nests are often located in the tops of evergreens, which also makes them hard to spot.

The best time to discover a nest is when the young are several days old and start to call as the parents bring them food. From then on, the older they get, the louder they get. When the nestlings receive food, their caws change to garbled sounds that make it seem as if they are strangling, although they obviously aren't. These feeding calls continue far into summer. After that, the young feed on their own.

Bird Feeder Journal

June 10, 10 A.M. The crows were making a racket in the woods, and when we looked out our study window we saw a hawk swoop down over the feeder. It was an immature Cooper's hawk, and it didn't seem very good at catching birds. The crows and other birds seemed to know this and even continued to feed with the hawk perched nearby.

December 18, 6:30 A.M. It is pretty clear that we have two separate groups of crows on our property and that they are staying distinct throughout winter. One group has seven birds, the other five. Each morning they arrive at the ground feeder, caw at each other, chase each other, and vie for dominance over the feeder. The two groups never feed together.

American crow. A large all-black bird with a large bill and dark eye. The male and female look alike.

American crow range map

EVENING GROSBEAK

Evening Grosbeak / *Coccothraustes vespertinus*

Expanding Range

Evening grosbeaks were relatively unknown until about 1850, for they were primarily a western bird. Then in 1854 they were seen in Toronto. Their numbers gradually increased in the northern Midwest, and by 1887 evening grosbeaks had been recorded in Ontario, Indiana, and Kentucky. In the winter of 1889–1890 there was a great eastward expansion, and they reached the coast of Massachusetts. They have also increased the range of their summer breeding grounds.

One of the reasons for this expansion is the widespread planting of the popular shade tree called box elder or ash-leaved maple (*Acer negundo*). This tree produces lots of seeds that evening grosbeaks particularly enjoy. Another explanation is the larger number of bird feeders that supply sunflower seed, also a favorite food.

Now You See Them, Now You Don't

People are often mystified about why evening grosbeaks seem to mob their feeders some years and other years are surprisingly scarce. It is important to remember that different birds have very different winter habits and social structures, often related to their food source. A pair of nuthatches may be seen at your feeder throughout the year, because they live in a fixed home range and eat insects found on trees. There is enough food to support a pair throughout the year. Evening grosbeaks, in contrast, remain in flocks and feed on tree seeds. The production of tree seeds varies from year to year and region to region, making fixed winter distribution patterns impossible. Instead, evening grosbeaks have to move about to take advantage of local seed abundance.

Watching Grosbeaks Feed

Besides having a great fondness for sunflower seeds at our feeders, evening grosbeaks eat a variety of other seeds, buds, and fruits. They eat the seeds of the box elder tree with great skill, manipulating the seed between their powerful beak and quickly extracting the seed as the winged pod flutters to the ground. They eat the seeds of many other kinds of trees — including those of sugar maples, pines, and tulip poplars — and will nip off and eat the buds of elms and other trees and shrubs. When they eat fruit, such as cherries, they can be heard crushing the cherry stones with their powerful mandibles. They will eat snow and the sap from trees, and they are attracted to the road salt that is left on gravel and sand after the winter.

Their Bills Change Color

The heads of male evening grosbeaks have such striking plumage that a friend of ours has likened them to space helmets and calls the birds space cadets. Some people say they look like oversized goldfinches.

In early spring an amazing thing happens: Their beaks turn from yellow to a beautiful light green. Look at the birds through your binoculars to get a good view of this; it is a gorgeous sight. The birds are also dimorphic, meaning that male and female look different. The male is darker on his head with bright yellow around his black wings; the female has more muted colors all over and lacks the bright yellow around the wings.

Behavior at Your Feeder

When the grosbeaks arrive, it is a mixed blessing, for they can eat large quantities of sunflower seed and be a dominating bird at the feeder. However, they are stunning to look at, and their beautiful

Evening grosbeak, male. A medium-sized bird with black wings and tail, yellowish body, and a yellow streak across its forehead and eye.

Evening grosbeak range map

Evening grosbeak, female. A medium-sized bird with black wings and tail, a grayish tan body, and no yellow streak across its forehead or eye.

"sleigh-bell" calls are a joy to hear. They seem to prefer feeders with ledges, tray-type feeders, or seed on the ground. When feeding on the open ground, they are more harmonious; when a number of them crowd together, as on a feeding tray, they can be very aggressive, opening their beaks and lunging at one another. It is interesting to see which birds are dominant.

Evening grosbeaks may linger at feeders until May before returning north to breed, and at this time you may see some of their courtship behavior. Males feed females as part of their courtship. The female or male may bob or sway in front of the other, or the female may quiver her wings and give short calls as she receives food. Males have another elaborate display in which they spread and vibrate their wings and pivot back and forth. Look for these behaviors at your feeder in spring.

Bird Feeder Journal

January 18, 8:30 A.M. It snowed hard last night. There are thirty evening grosbeaks at the feeder; the numbers have been climbing since they arrived last November 23. Males and females are crowded together on the ledge of the hanging house feeder, constantly competing for space.

April 4, 10 A.M. Eighteen evening grosbeaks flew overhead. Their beaks have changed from yellow to the most incredible pale jade green. Yesterday at our feeder ten were crowded on the platform, and we saw a male put sunflower seeds in a female's beak three times!

FINCHES

Purple Finch / *Carpodacus purpureus*

House Finch / *Carpodacus mexicanus*

Which Finch? House or Purple?

Purple finches and house finches are both in the genus *Carpodacus* and thus are close relatives. They have similar songs, breeding behaviors, and appearances, and people often are confused as to which they have at their feeders. Distinguishing between the two species can be difficult due to individual variation within each species. We get both at our feeders, and so we enjoy this challenge all the time.

The females are easier to tell apart than the males. Look at their heads. The female purple finch has a *broad white eyebrow stripe,* while the female house finch has *no distinct markings on her head,* which is completely covered with fine brown streaks.

The best clues to distinguishing the males are on their heads and flanks (the sides of their belly). The male purple finch is *raspberry red* all over his head, back, rump, and breast, and he has *faint or no brown streaks* along his flanks. The *red or orange-red* of the male house finch is limited, falling mainly on his forehead, chest, and rump; he has *thick brown streaks* along his flanks.

In general, purple finches are somewhat larger and stockier than house finches and have a more pronounced notch at the tip of their tails.

You should know that male purple finches in their first year have no red plumage and look much like the female. Not until their second year do they acquire the red color.

Do They Get Brighter in Spring?

If it looks to you as if male purple and house finches are a brighter red in spring than they were all fall

House finch, male. A small brownish bird with orange-red over the eye and on the breast and heavy brown streaking along the flanks.

House finch, female. A small brown bird, heavily streaked on the breast and finely streaked on the head.

House finch range map

and winter, you are absolutely right. However, this brighter plumage is not acquired through a late winter molt, for these birds have only one molt per year, and that is in late summer and fall. Rather, their red feathers are tipped with gray after their fall molt, and the gray wears off by spring to reveal the brighter colors underneath.

"Hollywood Finches"

House finches are native to the western states, and although they are now common in the East, their presence there is a recent occurrence. In 1940 a few pet dealers in California captured house finches and shipped them to New York City to be sold as "Hollywood finches." Catching and shipping the birds were illegal, and when agents of the U.S. Fish and Wildlife Service discovered the scheme, they began to arrest the New York dealers who had the birds. To avoid being arrested, some dealers released the house finches, and the birds survived and reproduced in the wild. They have now spread throughout most of the eastern states, and their population is still growing.

Songs and Calls

House finch song occurs most often in spring and summer, but bits of it may be heard on the warmer days of fall and winter. Both male and female give song, a long series of musical warblings usually end-

ing with a harsh "chee-urr." This last harsh sound will help you distinguish house finch song from the similar song of the purple finch. Purple finch song is a long musical warbling similar to that of the house finch, but it does not have the harsh note at the end, and it is given only by the male.

The normal call note of the house finch sounds just like the "cheerp" of a house sparrow. The normal call note of the purple finch, given as the birds are in flight, is a short, metallic "tick" that is distinctive.

Feeder Habits

Both finches generally remain in small flocks through winter, and both are attracted to seeds at feeders, especially sunflower seed. In the wild, house finches feed on seeds from trees and weeds and are comfortable feeding at hanging or ground feeders. The purple finch is more accustomed to feeding on tree seeds — such as those of conifers, sycamores, elms, and the buds and flowers of fruit trees — and may be more used to feeding above the ground.

Habitat Habits

House finches are very comfortable around urban dwellings and live in both the city and suburbs. They will also breed in these areas, since they are willing to place their nest just about anywhere. Once nest-

Purple finch, male. A small bird with raspberry red on its head, back, breast, and belly, and little or no brown streaking on its flanks.

Purple finch range map

Purple finch, female. A small brown bird with a white eye stripe and sparse streaking on the breast.

ing is over, both young and adults tend to go to areas where there are abundant seeds to feed on; thus, they may be less prevalent at this time. But during winter or summer they remain in the same general area, for they migrate only a short distance or not at all.

The purple finch is less of a city bird, preferring to nest in mixed woods or conifers. It breeds along the West Coast, across Canada, and in the northeastern states. In fall it migrates south for the winter and may visit feeders anywhere in the eastern United States. However, it cannot be counted on as a winter visitor, for flocks will stop and stay at any available food on their way rather than head for a certain spot each year, as most other winter birds do.

In certain years there are large influxes of purple finches farther south. This is probably due to a lack of food in the North.

Bird Feeder Journal

April 28, 10 A.M. A male house finch just took a hulled sunflower seed from the feeder and fed it to the female, which was perched nearby.

July 16, 3:30 P.M. Ten house finches were gathered on our garden path. One started to sunbathe by crouching down with tail and wings spread over the ground and its body tilted to one side. Soon four others joined in the sunbathing, while the other five finches pecked at things on the ground. Sunbathing lasts for about one minute. The path is covered with wood chips, and interestingly, other species of birds have sunbathed in the same spot at other times.

GOLDFINCH

American Goldfinch / *Carduelis tristis*

Watching Goldfinches Feed

If you watch goldfinches at your feeder, you will immediately notice that they feed in a very different manner than many other birds. Chickadees and titmice, for instance, come to the feeder, take a single seed, and fly off. But goldfinches land on the feeder and continue to eat seed after seed. This method may stem from their eating habits in the wild, where they land on a composite flower head or a birch and eat many seeds right at that spot.

Watch them closely and you will notice that they can take off the outer hull of a seed while keeping it in their bill and do not depend on holding it in their feet and pecking at it like the chickadees. They are able to do this because the conical shape of their bill is specially adapted for seed eating. This bill shape is typical of all finches, such as house finches, purple finches, and evening grosbeaks.

What They Eat

In the wild, you will find goldfinches feeding wherever there are lots of seeds; generally they take seeds right off a plant rather than feeding on ones that have fallen below. They like to feed on birch seeds and alder seeds in winter, and in spring through fall they eat composite weed seeds such as thistle, sunflower, dandelion, ragweed, mullein, evening primrose, and goldenrod. Go out and watch what they feed on and see if you can identify it.

At feeders, goldfinches are partial to sunflower and thistle seeds. They prefer hulled over regular sunflower, so if you want to dispense with the more expensive thistle seed you can still attract plenty of goldfinches with sunflower.

Spring Singing

Some spring morning you will walk outside and hear constant singing and chirping from the treetops near your feeder. The singing sounds like a flock of canaries, but it is actually goldfinches (there is no relationship between the two), and they are starting some of their breeding behavior. Their song is a long warbling sound lasting thirty seconds or more. Nobody knows the function of this singing nor why it starts so far ahead of breeding.

The Goldfinch-Thistle Myth

It is often stated that goldfinches do not nest until the thistles have bloomed and gone to seed because the goldfinch needs the thistle down for its nest. This is not true; goldfinches often build nests long before thistle is in bloom, for they can use all types of other fibers in their nests. We have seen them build with fibers from milkweed stalks, salsify seed tops, and other downy materials.

The reason for goldfinches' late nesting (starting in July) is probably that they feed their young on the seeds of composite flowers, such as thistle or sunflower, which ripen in late summer.

American goldfinch, male, in spring and summer. A small bright yellow bird with black wings and tail, white wing bars, and a black patch on its forehead.

American goldfinch, female, in spring and summer. A small bird with a yellow breast, brownish olive black, black wings and tail, and white wing bars.

American goldfinch range map

Changing Colors

Goldfinches molt twice a year. In fall, after breeding, they have a complete molt. At this time the male, which in summer is bright yellow and has a black patch over his bill, loses these colors and grows in feathers that look like a grayish version of the summer female. The female also changes from her bright yellow plumage of summer into this grayer color. Thus in winter it is impossible to distinguish between male and female goldfinches.

In spring, goldfinches molt all their body feathers but not their wing feathers. At this time both acquire their summer plumage. The male's brighter color may help him attract a female or advertise the boundaries of his territory, while the female's more camouflaged coloration may allow her to be more secretive around the nest.

American goldfinch, male or female, in fall and winter. A small bird with a grayish yellow or brownish yellow body, and black wings and tail. The wings are marked with a conspicuous white bar.

Bird Feeder Journal

January 5, 2 P.M. A flock of about twenty-five goldfinches has been visiting our feeder over the past two weeks. They are aggressive at the perches, for they cannot all fit on at once. When they start feeding, the seed level in our hanging feeder starts dropping at an alarming rate!

August 25, 3 P.M. We watch young goldfinches eating at the feeder and then flying off with their father to a nearby tree, where they are fed by him as well. Their fledgling calls of "chipeee chipeee chipeee" are distinctive and can be heard whenever they fly after their parents.

GRACKLE

Common Grackle / *Quiscalus quiscula*

Looking at the Sky?

Watch the grackles at your feeder, and every so often you will see them point their bills up as if they were looking at the sky. They are not really looking at the sky, for when birds do that they tilt their head to one side. The grackles are performing a display called bill tilt that is part of grackle language. It is usually done between two males or two females when they are competing for dominance over a mate or at a feeding site. The display is held for several seconds, and then the birds resume feeding. Bill-tilting is especially likely to occur when new birds arrive on the scene.

Identifying Male, Female, and Juvenile

Male and female grackles look similar in that they are both black with iridescent heads. However, the male is larger, has a longer tail, and has more iridescence. There are several other tricks for telling them apart. During the breeding season the female is almost always in the lead when the two fly. Also, a flying male, especially just after takeoff and just before landing, folds his tail vertically into a V. This is a display done only during the breeding period, and it may advertise the bird's sex and breeding readiness to other grackles.

The first young grackles are seen in late spring and early summer. They can be identified by their dark-brown plumage (different from the black of the adults) and their dark eye, which is strikingly unlike the bright yellow iris of the adults.

Searching for the Ruff-Out

The song of grackles will never make the record books as most melodious, for it sounds like a squeaky gate. It is given by the male or female and is often written as "reedeleek," "scoodeleek," or "ch'gasqueek." Males often sing when near other males, and paired males and females may alternate singing.

One thing to look for when the male or female is singing is a visual display called ruff-out. In this display the bird spreads its tail, opens its wings a little bit, and ruffles out its head and body feathers. Part of what the ruff-out does is heighten the effect of the iridescence on the bird's feathers, and it is always accompanied by song.

Looking for Nests

Soon after they arrive on their breeding grounds and are seen at your feeder, grackles will begin breeding behavior. Look for signs of nest-building. Grackles often nest in surburban areas, and they usually choose evergreens in which to build. A good clue is seeing the male or female flying into these spots with long strands of grass trailing from its beak. This is a preliminary stage of grackle nest-building, done sporadically and lasting from one to four weeks. These grasses are not used in building the nest that the birds ultimately use, and it is not known why grackles transport them to the nest site.

After this stage, the real nest-building takes place, and it is all done by the female; the male merely follows her around. The nest may be placed where the strands of grass were laid. It is constructed in about five days, contains grasses and mud, and looks like a large version of a robin's nest.

Strange Antics

Grackles have several unusual behaviors that people often see around their feeders or in their yards. One is the occasional killing of other small birds, especially house sparrows. Some people have actually seen them drown house sparrows in the bird-

Common grackle, male.
A medium-sized black bird with a bright yellow eye. The male has a long tail and iridescence on the feathers; the female (not pictured) has a shorter tail and less iridescence.

Common grackle range map

bath. Generally just one individual in a given area picks up this behavior, but in any case it is startling.

Another behavior is referred to as anting. Here the grackle rubs different materials over its feathers, possibly to rid itself of feather parasites or to soothe its skin. Sometimes the bird uses ants, and thus the name of the behavior. The ants may be squeezed and rubbed through the feathers, releasing formic acid, or the bird may spread its feathers over the ants and let them crawl about. In other cases birds may use different substances for anting, such as mothballs or cigarette butts. Many other species of birds practice anting, but grackles are most often seen doing it.

A third unusual habit involves feeding. Grackles are often seen taking some kind of food — crackers, stale bread, even dry dog food — and carrying it to water, such as a birdbath, where they soak it before eating it. Occasionally food "prepared" in this way is fed to fledglings.

Bird Feeder Journal

October 14, 4 P.M. Hundreds of grackles have temporarily descended into our woods and are feeding on the ground. Their noise is astoundingly loud. The birds are walking through the woods and flipping over leaves in search of insects or other food. Every so often they all suddenly fly up and silently perch in the trees. Then gradually they drop down to feed again and continue their raucous sounds. A spectacular sight.

June 1, 5 P.M. The first young grackles for the year have shown up at the feeder. They are brownish and have dark eyes. They are not feeding on their own yet but just following the parents to the feeder and then soliciting food from the parents even though it is right in front of them, free for the taking. They make a harsh, grating sound and flutter their wings as they receive food.

HOUSE SPARROW

House Sparrow / *Passer domesticus*

Which Is Male, Which Is Female?

Although house sparrows are one of our most common birds, few people know that there are easy ways to distinguish between the male and female. Knowing the sexes of the birds will add to your enjoyment as you watch them and will help you interpret interactions you might see.

To tell male from female, look at the face and chin of the bird. The male has black around the eye and under the chin, while the female has beige around the eye and is all gray under the chin. In spring and summer, the male's bill is black and the female's yellow. In winter they both have yellowish bills.

Winter Coat Wearing Thin

House sparrows have one complete molt of all their feathers each year, in late summer. Right after the molt the tips of their feathers are lined with a buffy edge, and the black bib of the male is partially concealed by white tips at the ends of its feathers. Look for this in fall.

Over the winter the white tips on the black chin feathers of the male gradually wear off so that by spring, when breeding is about to start, his bib is large and glossy black. At about this same time, watch to see his bill change color. In winter it is yellowish like that of the female, but in spring it becomes dark black and blends with his black bib.

It's Not a Sparrow

Actually, the house sparrow is not related to our other sparrows at all; in fact, it is not a sparrow but belongs to a group of birds called weaver finches or weaverbirds, which are native to Eurasia and Africa. They get their name from their habit of weaving plant fibers together into a spherical nest (as does the house sparrow) or a hanging nest. This is different from our true sparrows, which build cup-like nests of grasses.

Although this bird's correct common name is "house sparrow," it is often called English sparrow because it was originally introduced into North America from England.

Daily Movements

If you watch the behavior of house sparrows in fall and winter, you will notice that two times each day they form tight little flocks. Around noon they gather in bushes or low shrubbery for about an hour, preening and chirping. These flocks are noisy and conspicuous, and why the birds gather like this is not known. It may be simply a resting and digesting period during which the birds are safer in a flock.

Again in late afternoon, various flocks join together, with many of the birds chirping loudly. As it gets dark they gradually travel to a nearby roost, which is usually either some dense shrubbery, trees, ivy-covered walls, or a protected structure like a bridge. In the morning they all leave.

In summer and spring the birds are more closely

House sparrow, male. A small brown bird with an unstreaked breast and black around the eye and chin.

House sparrow, female. A small brown bird with an unstreaked breast and a buffy eye stripe.

House sparrow range map

associated with their nests and may roost in the nest hole or near the nest site.

Watching Nest-Site Behavior

House sparrow nests can be anywhere there is a cavity large enough to stuff with grasses and other fibrous materials. In the city you often find house sparrows building in the letter of a large sign, at the edge of an awning, around an air conditioner, in a traffic light, or in the eaves of a building. In the country they use tree holes or birdhouses and occasionally build a spherical nest among tree branches.

The behavior of the birds at the nest site is fun to watch. An unmated male usually perches near his prospective nest site and advertises his presence through a repeated call that sounds like "chirup-chireep-chirup." He does this almost incessantly until a female comes near, at which point he calls faster and louder and quivers his wings. If the female shows some interest, the male may go in and out of his nest hole several times in front of her. If the female also enters the nest hole, there is a good chance the two will pair.

The nest is usually a sphere with an entrance on the side. Both birds will bring long strands of nesting material to the site and share in the building, although an unmated male may do some initial build-

ing alone. It is interesting to watch them collect material, which includes string, grass, leaves, paper, and feathers.

"Introducing . . . "

The house sparrow is not native to North America. The first birds were brought from England to Brooklyn, New York, in 1850. They were unsuccessful at breeding, but with repeated introductions in the next few years they became established. The bird was originally introduced with the intention of reducing the number of certain insect pests. Although the birds unfortunately did not help with those particular insects, they did eventually multiply rapidly. There were many more introductions in various parts of North America, and by 1900 house sparrows were the most common bird in North America and were even more numerous than they are today. Being aggressive birds, they took over many of the nest holes of native species such as tree swallows, bluebirds, and house wrens.

But from about 1915 to 1920 house sparrow populations started to decline, resulting in the population level that we have today. This decline was probably due to the introduction of the automobile and the subsequent drop in demand for horses as a means of transportation. With fewer horses in the towns and cities, there was less grain left over from their feed and in their droppings. House sparrows depended greatly on these sources of grain to live on in winter, and without them, many died.

Bird Feeder Journal

May 3, 9 A.M. The nest box above the garage doors has house sparrows building in it. But strangely, there are two females and one male attending the box. The females are aggressive to each other, but the male tolerates both. When one female is in the box, the other perches on top. We wonder if this is a case of polygamy.

August 20, 4 P.M. Lots of young house sparrows are frequenting our feeder in flocks, especially in the afternoon. This seems to happen each year at this time. It is mostly young birds. Within a few weeks they usually stop coming; they must feed elsewhere for the rest of the winter and then disperse to their breeding grounds in spring.

HUMMINGBIRDS

Rufous Hummingbird / *Selasphorus rufus*   Anna's Hummingbird / *Calypte anna*

Ruby-Throated Hummingbird / *Archilochus colubris*

Black-Chinned Hummingbird / *Archilochus alexandri*

Tiny Marvels

We will never forget our first look at a hummingbird in our garden. Determined to attract hummingbirds, we had bought and planted cardinal flower, and we waited impatiently for it to bloom. As if on cue, when the first blossom opened, a ruby-throated hummingbird appeared. We were thrilled to see this tiny bundle of energy zip from one blossom to another. With our binoculars we focused in and noticed that its forehead was a bright yellow, and for one fleeting second we thought that we had a rare kind of hummingbird in our garden. Then we realized that its forehead was coated with yellow pollen! Oblivious to its role in the important work of cross-pollination, the hummingbird continued to visit each flower and drink the nectar.

These tiny marvels amaze us with so many features — their jewel-like colors, their fantastic flying abilities, and their size (a ruby-throat weighs $\frac{1}{10}$ of an ounce and is only 3¾ inches long).

There are sixteen species of hummingbirds that breed in the United States. In the East, there is only the ruby-throated hummingbird, although on rare occasions one of the western species has been seen. West of the Mississippi, some of the common hummingbirds that come to feeders are the black-chinned, rufous, and Anna's hummingbirds.

Winged Jewels

The iridescence on hummingbirds' feathers makes them sparkle like jewels and covers only the outer third of the feather. When light strikes these feathers, it is reflected and intensified when viewed

Ruby-throated hummingbird, male. A tiny bird with a long bill, green back, and whitish belly. The male has an iridescent red throat that may appear black in certain light.

Ruby-throated hummingbird range map

from a certain angle. That is why, for example, a male ruby-throated hummingbird's throat patch will appear to be brilliant red if the light is shining directly on it. When viewed from a different angle it will look dusky orange, green, or violet, and when no light is reflected it will look black.

Living Helicopters

Hummingbirds can fly in every direction: up, down, sideways, and even upside down, which they may do briefly to escape. When they are hovering, their wings move backward and forward, rotating at the shoulder, and the tips trace a horizontal figure eight.

Hummers are among the fastest small birds, reaching speeds of 60 miles per hour in forward flight. They can also fly long distances in their migration to Central America, including 500 miles across the Gulf of Mexico. Fortunately, an adult ruby-throat can store up to 2 grams of fat, enough to make this over-water crossing.

Red Is Their Favorite Color

Someone once said, "Hummingbirds like any color, as long as it's red." We have actually seen them at flowers of every color, including the greenish yellow flowers of the buckthorn shrub, but they do have a preference for red flowers. Hummingbirds are not born with this preference but learn through trial and error that red means good food.

Many of these red flowers have special adaptations to lure hummingbirds. They offer quantities of nectar with just the concentration of sugar that hummingbirds prefer, about 20 to 25 percent. The hummingbirds, in turn, provide a valuable service to the flowers — that of cross-pollination.

Their preference for red explains why hummingbirds will explore almost any red object, including hummingbird feeders, red floral patterns on fabric, red hair ribbons, and even sunburned noses! It is interesting to us that the brightest iridescent colors on hummingbirds are so often red or in the red spectrum. Perhaps this helps them find one another.

Eating Nectar

Hummingbirds have a higher metabolism than any other bird and must eat enormous amounts of food to fuel themselves. Nectar is an easily digested

Ruby-throated hummingbird, female, at nest. A tiny bird with a long bill, green back, and whitish belly. The female has a whitish throat.

source of quick energy for hummers. It has been estimated that they consume 50 percent of their weight in sugar each day. Hummingbirds also need proteins, fats, and minerals, and they get these by eating small insects and spiders that they find on the flowers they visit or on other vegetation. When a hummer visits a flower, it collects the nectar by drawing its tongue in and out of the flower about thirteen times per second.

To save energy when feeding, a hummer will perch instead of hover if it can. A male ruby-throat in our garden perched on the stakes supporting the delphiniums when he visited that plant. Hummingbirds can save energy at night, particularly when it is cold, by going into a state of torpor. Their metabolic rate drops to one-fifth of normal, their heartbeat and breathing slow down, and their body temperature becomes lower.

Anna's hummingbird, female. A tiny bird with a green back, an occasional trace of red on the throat, and grayish underparts covered by varying amounts of green.

Anna's hummingbird, male. A tiny bird whose entire head and throat are covered with iridescent red, which in certain lights may appear dark.

Anna's hummingbird range map

Aerial Acrobatics

The famous aerial acrobatics of hummingbirds are visual displays that serve to defend a territory, attract a mate, or intimidate other hummingbirds (or sometimes people near their feeder). Each species of hummingbird has flight patterns that are unique to that species.

In its visual display, a male ruby-throated hummingbird flies along a wide, shallow arc, as though suspended by a wire. He usually is oriented toward the sun so that its rays reflect his iridescent red throat. He may pass close to the female, and his wings and tail will produce a loud buzzing at that point. Sometimes a male and female ruby-throat hover in the air, facing one another, and move up and down, either in unison or alternately. One observer saw them mate on the ground after such displaying.

The male Anna's hummingbird defends a territory around a rich food source. When displaying, the male will rise up more than 150 feet, pause, sing (a thin grinding sound) briefly, and then zoom down over the female, making a loud popping noise as he swoops over her. This noise may be made by his tail feathers.

Black-chinned male hummingbirds display by flying back and forth in a shallow 3-foot-long arc. The rufous hummingbird is very aggressive when defending feeding or nesting territories. Its display flight is a diagonal loop, and it moves faster going down and more slowly going up, accompanied by a loud whirring of its wings.

Tiny Nests

A female builds a nest and then seeks out a mate. After mating she lays two pinkish white eggs and raises the young alone. The nestlings will remain in the nest for about twenty-one days as the mother feeds them regurgitated nectar and insects. She will fiercely defend a territory around her nest from intruding hummers and occasionally other birds.

Hummingbird nests are the tiniest in the bird world, no bigger than a half-dollar. They usually blend in so beautifully with their surroundings that they can be impossible to spot. The nests may be adorned with such materials as insect cocoons, fern scales, spider skeletons, and lichen. They are flexible enough to actually stretch as the baby hummingbirds grow.

At Your Feeder

Depending on the area of the country that you live in, you may attract one or several species of hummingbirds and many individuals of each species. Hummers can be fiercely competitive over food sources, and you may see much aggressive behavior among them as they compete for feeders or flowers. They will swoop and dive at one another and may make a variety of clicking or buzzing sounds. You may also find that some hummers seem to be at the feeder frequently, while others visit briefly and then leave, often using the same entrance and exit route each time. Most hummingbirds will also spend a considerable amount of time perching, often on favorite bare branches overlooking the garden.

Bird Feeder Journal

June 21, 5 P.M. The male ruby-throat flies down to the flowers about every twenty minutes and feeds for only two minutes, favoring the coral-bells and the delphiniums. He returns each time to the same perch, with his back to the sun. He preens his wings and breast with his bill and then reaches his foot over his wing to scratch at and preen the feathers under his chin that his bill can't reach.

Black-chinned hummingbird, male. A tiny bird with a green back, black chin, and a line of iridescent violet just below the chin that shows only in good lighting. The female looks much like the female ruby-throated hummingbird.

Black-chinned hummingbird range map

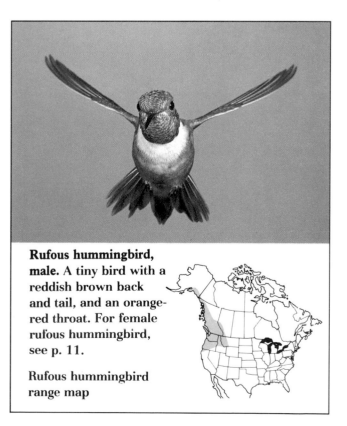

Rufous hummingbird, male. A tiny bird with a reddish brown back and tail, and an orange-red throat. For female rufous hummingbird, see p. 11.

Rufous hummingbird range map

JAYS

Blue Jay / *Cyanocitta cristata*

Scrub Jay / *Aphelocoma coerulescens*

Beautiful Bird

The blue jay is one of the most beautiful of our feeder birds. Its colors are particularly brilliant in fall and early winter, possibly because it has just undergone its yearly molt in late summer and all its feathers are fresh. At this time the black barring and bright white spots stand out against the blue of the back, tail, and wing feathers. You could easily spend a lot of money traveling to the tropics to see a bird this stunning. Why not enjoy it right at home?

Look for Courtship

Have you ever noticed on a sunny day in late winter that the blue jays are suddenly more active and noisy? If you look for them on these mornings, you are likely to see flocks flying from tree to tree; once they land, they tend to hop higher and higher in the branches. They will be giving a great variety of calls: one is bell-like and sounds like "toolool, toolool"; another sounds like a squeaky gate, or "wheede-lee." The birds may also bob up and down. When the birds get to the top of the tree, they all fly off to another tree, calling "jaay, jaay," and then start over again. This behavior is believed to be blue jay courtship — a female in the lead and several males following and competing for her.

Another feature of blue jay courtship is called mate-feeding. It occurs in spring and summer and can be seen at your feeder. In mate-feeding the male picks up a seed, goes to the female, and feeds it to her. As she receives the seed she may fluff out her body feathers or rapidly flutter her wings, and she almost always gives a soft call that sounds like "kueu, kueu, kueu" or "kuetkuetkuet."

Silent Time

We generally think of blue jays as always being raucous, but this is far from the truth. In fact, once their courtship is completed, paired birds become incredibly secretive as they build their nest and start to raise young. Look for these paired birds in midspring, when they are usually together, occasionally mate-feeding, and always moving quietly about within the cover of shrubbery. In fact, hearing the soft call of the female as she is fed may be your only clue to the birds' presence.

Once the young are born, you will begin to hear more calls from the parents and nestlings.

An interesting characteristic of the blue jay is its ability to imitate the calls of hawks. Jays in our yard mimic several different red-tailed hawk and broad-winged hawk calls. Sometimes there is a hawk in the area, usually circling overhead, when the jays give these calls. It is not known why jays do this.

Watching Jays Feed

We find that the best place to feed jays is at our large ground feeder. Generally, each jay defends its own personal distance of about a foot and will lunge at another jay that comes too close.

Jays feed on a wide variety of foods in the wild and sometimes fly off with extra food and store it. One of their favorite foods in fall and winter is acorns. They peck off the cap and then store or eat the rest of the nut. How many blue jays are around from year to year can be greatly affected by the abundance of acorns in previous years.

Blue Jay Myths

Blue jays are blamed for a lot of things. One is giving "false alarms" when they arrive at the feeder to scare other birds away and get more feed. While it is true that jays often call as they land at a feeder, this is probably not intended to scare away other birds, for they call even when no other birds are present. Other birds certainly pay attention to jay alarm calls, but they also pay attention to the alarm calls of all other species. If jays continually gave false alarms, the alarm would lose its effect over time.

Blue jays are also blamed for being aggressive to

Blue jay. A medium-sized bird with a blue head, back, wings, and tail, and a gray belly. It has a crest that may be raised or lowered. The male and female look alike.

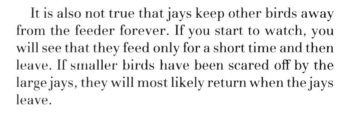

Blue jay range map

other birds while at the feeder. This is not unique to jays but is true of any bird that is larger than another. The best way to alleviate this is to have more space at the feeders. Our ground feeders are large, and jays can feed peacefully there with juncos and other birds.

It is also not true that jays keep other birds away from the feeder. If you start to watch, you will see that they feed only for a short time and then leave. If smaller birds have been scared off by the large jays, they will most likely return when the jays leave.

A Western Feeder Jay

The blue jay's range does not extend into the West, but in that region there are several other species of jays. These include the steller's jay, the gray jay, and the scrub jay. The scrub jay is the most common at feeders and in residential areas, the other two species remaining more in the woods and mountains. The scrub jay's behavior is similar in many ways to that of the blue jay: It has a wide variety of calls and social behaviors, and it feeds on an assortment of foods.

Scrub jay. A medium-sized bird with blue wings, tail, and head, a gray back and belly, and no crest. The male and female look alike.

Scrub jay range map

Bird Feeder Journal

December 30, 7 A.M. Twenty-five blue jays all feeding together at our ground feeder. Last year at this time we had only three or four. We have a local group of about six jays, and we have seen other small groups come here from neighboring areas about ¼ mile away. They seem to feed together with relatively little conflict.

JUNCO

Dark-Eyed Junco / *Junco hyemalis*

A Winter Visitor

Each fall we try to guess on which day the first dark-eyed juncos will arrive. These snowbirds, as some people call them, breed farther north of where we live in Massachusetts and come down into our area for the winter. Studies have shown that juncos usually return to the same winter area each year, so when they arrive we feel as if we are welcoming old friends; undoubtedly some of the birds are returning again from the previous year.

Our ground feeder was originally set up specifically to attract a junco flock, and within three days they had found and were using this feeder. If you do not have juncos, try setting up a ground feeder (see the chapter about ground feeders, p. 4), and then you can look forward to their arrival year after year.

Who's the Boss?

Junco flocks have an interesting and complex social arrangement. Male juncos tend to winter farther north than female juncos, so the farther north you are, the higher will be the proportion of males in your junco flock. In a winter flock, males usually dominate females, and adults of both sexes tend to dominate first-year birds.

Once the winter flock has arrived, the members form a social hierarchy that remains stable for the winter. This means there is one top bird that is dominant over all the others, then a second-ranked bird, and so on down the line. Chickadees have a similar winter social organization.

If you watch juncos at your feeder, you can often tell which birds are dominant just by their behavior. A dominant bird will fly or run at another bird as if it were going to peck it, making the other bird move away. Occasionally a subordinate bird will resist, and the two birds will face each other and raise and lower their heads. Fights are rare but do occur; two birds will fly vertically up to 10 feet and claw at each other.

The junco flock will remain in a defined foraging

area all winter. You will not see all of the members of the flock at once, because they do not travel together all the time. You are more likely to see them together in bad weather, when they frequent the feeder more often.

Junco Calls

Juncos make a variety of sounds during interactions. Go outside to observe your junco flock, and you will be able to hear their sounds. At a feeder they usually give a "zeet" call when arriving and a "tsip" when they leave. During dominance interactions, they often give "kew, kew, kew" calls.

A Change in Behavior

In late winter, look for a change in junco behavior. There will be more chases between birds in which

Dark-eyed junco, male. A small bird, all dark on its upper half and white below, with a light-colored bill. The male is all dark gray above.

56

Dark-eyed junco, female. It is similar to the male, but the dark parts of her body have more brown in them.

Dark-eyed junco range map

they flash their white outer tail feathers. The males will start to sing more frequently. Their song is a musical trill, and many people confuse it with the song of a chipping sparrow. Go out and listen to the singing and see if there is a difference among individual songs. We found this to be true.

This changed behavior is a sign that the breeding season is approaching, even though the juncos have not quite yet left your feeders. One day you will look out and realize that they are gone, but you may hardly notice it because you are paying attention to the new spring arrivals. The juncos will have returned to their breeding grounds.

Identifying Juncos

Juncos' plumage varies in different areas of the country, which originally led scientists to name four species of juncos. Now they are all considered one species, the dark-eyed junco.

In the East, juncos (formerly called slate-colored juncos) are dark gray above and white underneath. In general, adult males tend to have all dark-gray upperparts with no brown; females and immature birds (first-year males and females) have varying amounts of brown.

In the western junco (formerly called Oregon junco), males have black hoods and reddish brown backs and sides; females are drabber and browner. There is a pink-sided form of this junco in the Rocky Mountains.

In the Black Hills area, in South Dakota and Wyoming, juncos (formerly called white-winged juncos) are bluish gray above and white below, with two white wing bars.

In the southern Rocky Mountains, juncos (formerly called gray-headed juncos) are pale gray with bright reddish brown backs.

Bird Feeder Journal

March 31, 3:30 P.M. There are six juncos at the feeder. A chipmunk is feeding peaceably near them. Two juncos come close and alternately raise and lower their heads to one another and make a "chip, chip, chip, kew, kew, kew" sound all strung together. Something frightens the flock, and they all fly into the brush pile, giving "tsip" sounds.

April 1, 5:10 P.M. Juncos have been singing more and more. At sundown, they went from our feeder to a nearby field, and there was much singing and chasing. They finally went to roost for the night in a very bushy spruce tree. We cautiously peered into the branches but could not see them. There were lots of droppings on the branches, a sign that this was a much-used spot.

MOCKINGBIRD

Northern Mockingbird / *Mimus polyglottos*

Mocking Mystery

If you are good at identifying bird songs, you can have a lot of fun listening to a mockingbird sing, for it can mimic the songs and calls of all other birds. Mockingbirds can even mimic other sounds; we had one that imitated the call of an American toad, and there was one well-known bird in California that imitated the fire sirens from a nearby station.

Amazingly, the mockingbird has no distinct song of its own but only imitates the songs of others. This habit is shared by its close relatives the gray catbird and brown thrasher. Interestingly, each of these three birds tends to repeat the songs of other birds a different number of times — the catbird sings them once, the thrasher twice, and the mockingbird three or more times.

Nobody has yet figured out why these birds act as mimics. Some people have suggested that when a mockingbird sings other birds' songs, those birds may be fooled into thinking the area is already occupied and move elsewhere, thus leaving the mockingbird with more resources to itself. But this is only a guess.

Spring, Fall, and Night Songster

In spring, mockingbirds are very conspicuous as they sit in the tops of trees, on chimneys, or on telephone poles and sing loudly. At this time of year only the male sings; he is usually announcing his territory to other males and trying to attract a female. His nesting territory is about 1 to 2 acres. You will notice that as soon as he attracts a mate he stops singing, and the two begin building a nest and laying eggs.

In fall, mockingbirds start to sing again. This time both the male and female sing, so there is no way to tell them apart. They defend a territory of 1 to 2 acres that centers on a source of food, such as multiflora rose berries, which they will eat through the winter. The male and female may defend a territory together, or each may defend its own.

Mockingbirds may sing at night in either spring or fall, often when there is a full moon or if the bird lives near a street lamp.

Your Feeder Is in Its Territory!

Some people complain that they have a mockingbird chasing all other birds away from their feeder. This may occur in fall and winter if your feeder is in the mockingbird's fall and winter territory. The bird is usually defending not the feeder but a nearby bush or tree with berries on which it will feed throughout the winter. It chases other birds away, for it thinks they may eat its store of berries. The only solution is to move your feeder away from the berries and, hopefully, out of the bird's territory.

Interesting Actions

There are several unusual actions mockingbirds perform that people wonder about. One that occurs in spring is called loop flight. In between bouts of song delivered from a high perch, the bird flies up, makes a short loop, and then settles back on the perch. A lot of white on its wings and tail are conspicuous during the short flight, and the bird may even do a loop-the-loop. Loop flight is done by the male, and it usually serves to advertise his presence to possible mates and to other males that may have territories nearby.

Another behavior occurs in fall and is called border dance. Two birds face each other on the ground with heads and tails raised and hop back and forth and from side to side. This usually takes place at the common border of two neighboring birds and may help them agree on its location.

Finally there is wing-flashing, a display often given when the bird is on the ground. In it, the bird slowly raises its wings in a jerky fashion and then lowers them. Wing-flashing may occur while the bird is alone and feeding, or it may be given between dispersing immature birds and resident adults in fall. In the first case it may scare up insects as the

Watching Mockingbirds Feed

With the exception of hulled sunflower seed, mockingbirds are rarely attracted to the seed we put out for other birds. Instead they are attracted to fruits, such as apples and raisins, and also will eat suet or peanut butter if it is at a spot they can reach.

In the wild, mockingbirds tend to live wherever berries and fruits grow, and they especially like the fruits of multiflora rose and red cedar. Mockingbirds also eat a lot of insects, catching them on the ground or even occasionally in the air.

Northern mockingbird. A medium-sized bird, grayish above and lighter below, with a long tail and a small white patch on each wing. The patch is more visible when the bird is flying. The male and female look alike.

bird feeds; in the second case it may be an aggressive display. Its real function is still a mystery, so watch it closely for yourself and see if you can come up with your own theory.

Bird Feeder Journal

June 2, 8 A.M. Last night the male mockingbird next door was singing through much of the night. It has also been singing from conspicuous perches each day all spring. It has either lost its mate or never gotten one this year, for if it had, it would have stopped singing.

August 29, 11 A.M. Five or six mockingbirds just arrived in our field — perhaps young birds dispersing and looking for winter territories. The local mockingbirds are engaged in chasing them and in doing wing-flashing with the new birds. In the latter, two birds face each other, each stiffly raising and lowering its wings, and then one bird flies after the other.

A mockingbird at the nest with nestlings, who are waiting for a meal.

Northern mockingbird range map

MOURNING DOVE

Mourning Dove / *Zenaidura macroura*

Who's Mourning What?

People often think the name of this bird is spelled *morning dove*. Indeed, it is active early in the morning, but its name actually refers to its most common call, which has a mournful sound. It is given almost exclusively by the male in spring and summer and is a series of coos that sounds a lot like "ooahoo oo oo oo." The male mourning dove is in fact not mourning at all, but is trying either to attract a mate or defend a small area around his nest.

The only other call you will hear from mourning doves is a shortened version of the series of coos. It sounds like "ooahoo" and is most often given by the male as he calls the female to the nest site when the pair is choosing a site or actually building the nest. But it also can be given by male or female during courtship or territorial conflicts.

Large Crop / Loose Feathers

Mourning doves feed almost exclusively on small seeds that have fallen on the ground. They are fairly large birds, and though they are fast fliers when in the air, they are a bit slow on takeoff. This makes them vulnerable to predators such as sharp-shinned and Cooper's hawks, or cats, which may catch them while they feed.

Two adaptations of the mourning dove help protect it from predation. One is its large crop (the storage area in its throat), which enables it to take in large amounts of seeds in a short time and then retire to safety as it slowly releases the seeds into its stomach for digestion. The other adaptation is its loose feathers, which come out easily when the bird is grabbed by a predator. This often allows it to escape, leaving the predator with just a mouthful of feathers.

Watching Mourning Doves at Your Feeder

Whenever you have several mourning doves at your ground feeder, you are bound to see some interesting behavior. In winter you might see one bird run toward another while holding its head and tail in a horizontal plane, or you might see a bird quickly raise and lower one or both wings. These actions are performed by dominant birds in a flock and usually make other birds move away from choice feeding spots. Wing-raising may even be directed toward squirrels that are feeding too close to the dove; in these cases, the wing may be lowered so quickly that it makes a clapping sound.

In spring, when mourning doves are more involved with courtship, you will see different behavior. Males will run and hop short distances after females, bow down so their head touches the ground, lift up, puff out their chest, and give the call "ooahoo oo oo." You will see this throughout spring and summer at your ground feeder.

Watching Doves Away from Your Feeder

In fall and winter, you will notice that mourning doves alternate between feeding and retiring together to a nearby tree to sun, preen, and sit. During this time they are probably beginning to digest the large numbers of seeds they have just taken into their crop.

In spring and summer, mourning doves perform a lot of breeding behavior right near your feeder. Males and females perch together in pairs, and the male does what is known as perch-cooing: He sits erect, puffs out his iridescent throat feathers, bobs his tail, and gives the long coo, "ooahoo oo oo oo." He may also bow and coo in front of the female on the branch. She often moves a short distance away, and he follows. This can continue through most of

Mourning dove, adult. A medium-sized pigeon-like bird with a long tail, smooth beige head and breast, and gray wings and back. The adult has a black dot on the cheek. The male and female look similar.

Mourning dove, fledgling. Unlike the adult, the fledgling has no black dot on its cheek and has fine, buffy edgings to its wing feathers.

Mourning dove range map

the day. We see it for several months each summer in our yard.

Seeing Mourning Doves Mate

If you watch your mourning doves away from the feeder, you have a good chance of seeing them mate. There are several clues in their behavior that will help you know when the birds are going to mate. First you will see two birds perched right next to each other. Then one bird preens the head of the other, and they may hold each other's bills and bob their heads up and down. Next the male usually steps on the back of the female, and the two mate. After a few seconds he gets off her back, and both birds preen for a while before flying away. Copulation usually occurs on the male's territory, so the place where you see it occur is probably near the pair's nest.

Bird Feeder Journal

June 8, 2 P.M. A mourning dove is at the birdbath. It is drinking differently from other birds. Instead of taking a little bit of water and then tilting its head back to swallow, the mourning dove can actually sip up water through its bill. It keeps its bill in contact with the water as it drinks.

July 7, 11 A.M. A mourning dove near our ground feeder is sunbathing. It is lying down on one side with one wing totally spread out and its tail fanned. The bird looks as if it is in a trance. It has remained this way for more than five minutes. Now it is turning and spreading out the other wing, and its head is bent completely to one side. Five minutes later it flies to a branch and preens.

NUTHATCHES

White-Breasted Nuthatch / *Sitta carolinensis*

Red-Breasted Nuthatch / *Sitta canadensis*

Our Only Upside-Down Bird

One of the first things people notice about nuthatches is their ability to move headfirst down tree trunks. This enables them to find bits of food (insect larvae, for example) that "right-side up" birds, such as woodpeckers, may miss.

This ability is aided by the structure of the nuthatch's feet, which is different from that of many other birds. Most birds have four toes, three pointing forward and one pointing backward, but the nuthatch has two toes pointing forward and two pointing backward. Because of this, they can hold on better as they go down or up a tree trunk.

Down the Hatch

The name *nuthatch* comes from the old English word "nuthack," which referred to the bird's eating habits: When nuthatches eat a sunflower seed or a nut, they often wedge it into a bark crevice and hack it open. The bird could also have been named "nutstore," since it often takes food from the feeder and stores it in bark crevices for later use, even covering the stored food with a piece of bark or lichen. You can easily see them do this if you follow them when they leave your feeder.

We were once fascinated to see a nuthatch leave our feeder with a sunflower seed and store it in the bark of a pine. A junco was sitting in the same tree watching the nuthatch, and as soon as the nuthatch left, it went over and stole the sunflower seed. We have also seen titmice steal nuthatch stores.

Dictionary of Nuthatch Calls

"Ank ank" — This is given by male and female all year. When given as a simple "ank ank," it is usually a contact note between the pair. When given as a long series of rapid "anks," it is probably a response to some disturbance.

"Ip ip" — This is a very high, quiet sound given between the pair as they move about the woods,

feeding close together. It is a close-distance contact call that helps them keep track of each other.

"Werwerwerwer" — This rapid series of notes is the song of the male nuthatch. It is usually given from high in trees in late winter or spring when the birds are beginning their courtship.

Three's a Crowd

If you hear excited, rapid "ank" calls, go outside and you will probably see two or more nuthatches with their heads down and back feathers ruffled moving about near each other on a tree trunk. They may also spread their tails and slightly open their wings or chase after each other in flight. These are aggressive encounters between two males or two females in a spot where their ranges overlap.

Male and female nuthatches remain together through winter in an area of 25 to 45 acres. This is their range, and in spring, during breeding, they

White-breasted nuthatch, female. A small bird with a gray back, dark gray to silver cap, and white throat.

White-breasted nuthatch, male. It is similar to the female except its cap is jet black.

White-breasted nuthatch range map

Red-breasted nuthatch, male. A small bird with a gray back, a dark cap, a black line through the eye, and a light-reddish belly. The male has a darker cap and belly than the female (not pictured).

Red-breasted nuthatch range map

defend more aggressively a smaller portion of this as their territory. Ranges of neighboring nuthatches may overlap, and when the birds meet at these spots they are occasionally aggressive to each other. These encounters often involve a pair and a third bird, or two pairs.

You can distinguish male and female nuthatches by the extent and darkness of the black on their heads. On the male the black marking is jet black and large; on the female it is more limited and either all silver-gray or gray with blotches of black. Look for these differences, for they help you recognize pairs. In the southeastern states, these differences between male and female are less obvious or may not exist.

Early Courtship

Nuthatches can begin their courtship as early as January. On a clear morning you often can hear the male giving his song. In response, the female may approach and remain still as she perches nearby. After a while the two will go off and feed together for the day. At the end of the day, each goes to a separate hole in which to roost for the night.

Another engaging feature of nuthatch courtship is mate-feeding. The male collects a morsel of food,

flies to the female, and then places the food in her bill.

Red-Breasted and White-Breasted

Another nuthatch that may visit your feeder is the red-breasted nuthatch. The behavior of the two is very similar, but the sounds of the red-breasted are distinctive. Its most common sound is a nasal "meep meep."

In winter the red-breasted nuthatch moves south from its breeding grounds, which are mainly in the North.

Bird Feeder Journal

December 21, 4:30 P.M. We watched a male nuthatch choose his night roost hole in a bird box. We went out just as dusk was falling, and saw him at the feeder. With one last quiet "ip" call, he flew directly from the feeder to the box entrance and disappeared without a backward glance, snug and relatively safe for the night.

PIGEON

Pigeon / *Columba livia*

First Domesticated Bird

An animal is said to be domesticated when it has been bred by humans, lives under their care, is tame, and has been changed physically from its wild ancestors through selective breeding. It is believed that the pigeon is the first domesticated bird and that as early as 4500 B.C., in the Middle East, people may have raised pigeons for food. Their homing abilities were used to carry long-distance messages, such as results of battles or the outcome of early Olympic games. Pigeons were used as recently as World War II to carry messages.

As you look at pigeons you can see many variations in their colors. These are a result of selective breeding by people who wanted to show them for beauty or race them for sport.

Homing Ability

Homing is the ability of a bird to return to a known spot — its home — from various distances. Pigeons are able to home up to a thousand miles. Trainers sharpen this ability by releasing pigeons from increasingly longer distances from their home over a period of time. Sending a message by pigeon is not easy, since the message sender must first find a pigeon whose home is the same as the place where the message is to be delivered.

Any bird that migrates performs amazing feats of homing, for it makes long journeys between a wintering ground and a breeding ground each year. Much more still needs to be learned about the mechanics of homing, but studies of pigeons indicate that these birds use several methods of finding their way. Among them are remembering certain landmarks, orienting themselves to the sun and the stars, and even sensing the earth's magnetic field.

Fast Flight

Pigeons are among the best fliers in the bird world, and anyone who has watched them swoop around on the winds of a city street can appreciate this. They are also one of the fastest fliers, having been clocked at up to 82 miles per hour. Their excellent abilities are probably due to their original environment, along cliffs and rocky outcroppings, especially near the sea, where gusts of wind necessitated strong flight to land on the narrow cliff faces.

Such cliffs are also the habitat of the peregrine falcon, probably the fastest of all birds. Since the peregrine catches pigeons in midair for food, it may be that some of the pigeon's aerial skills have evolved to avoid the peregrine's attacks.

Flight Displays

Pigeons in normal flight are quiet and use strong, shallow wing beats, but around their nests they may execute a very different kind of flight. As they take off, they use deep wing beats, making their wings slap together in a clapping sound; once they are aloft they will alternate this clapping flight with glides in which their wings are held in a V over their back and their tail feathers are spread wide.

Look for this behavior around bridges and buildings where pigeons breed. It is performed most frequently by males and often stimulates other birds to do the same thing. Its function is not known.

Introduced to North America

Pigeons originally lived in Europe and the Middle East. They were probably first introduced into North America in 1606, in Nova Scotia. Over the next fifty years they were brought to both Massachusetts and Virginia, and now, of course, they can be found all across North America. They have flourished for several reasons: They are not disturbed by human activity or cars; they are generalists in their feeding behavior, surviving on the tidbits of food they find in cities; and buildings and bridges are so similar to their native nesting habitat of rock ledges that they readily accept them as nest sites.

Pigeon. A familiar medium-sized bird with various shades of gray, brown, or white on its feathers. There is a white marking at the base of the upper bill; iridescence on the neck shows in good light. The male and female look alike.

Pigeon range map

Watching Pigeons at Your Feeder

Whenever we see a group of pigeons feeding together, we take a moment to look at and enjoy several fascinating behaviors. One behavior is called bowing, and it usually occurs just after a bird has landed among other pigeons. The bird puffs out its neck feathers, lowers it head, and turns in half or full circles. Bowing is done most often by males that are asserting their dominance in front of other males or that are trying to attract a female.

Sometimes a bird that has been bowing in front of its mate continues into another behavior called tail drag, lifting its head high and dragging its spread tail feathers along the ground. It is a striking sight and can last for several seconds.

Finally, you may see two birds running in tandem through or away from the other feeding birds, one bird seeming to push the other along. This is called driving, and the male is behind the female. It may be done by the male to drive the female away from other males that he would have to compete with. Driving is very common.

City Birds

We do not have pigeons at our feeder, for we are not near enough to an urban center. But when we go to the city we always enjoy taking a moment to sit on a park bench and watch pigeon behavior. In large groups of pigeons there are always displays to be seen, and the birds are so used to humans you can get a good close look at their actions.

Next time you are in the city, take a moment to watch pigeon behavior; it is a fascinating occurrence that thousands of people walk by every day and never even notice.

PINE SISKIN

Pine Siskin / *Carduelis pinus*

One of the Flock

From fall through early spring, pine siskins remain in large flocks ranging in size from fifty to a thousand birds, with flocks of around two hundred birds being quite common. As the flock moves about to feed, it may join with other species, such as redpolls, goldfinches, and crossbills. These mixed flocks are not permanent associations but rather a result of birds being attracted to similar food sources, such as the seeds of birches and alders.

In spring, pine siskins become more aggressive toward each other; the large flocks begin to break up into smaller groups of five to ten birds. These flock sizes are retained even through the breeding season, for although a breeding pair defends a small area right around the nest, it may let other siskins land or nest in the same tree. And when the pair leaves the nest site, it often joins other siskins to feed. This strong orientation toward flocking is very similar to that of cedar waxwings, which also stay in flocks all year.

Aggression at Your Feeder

Pine siskins can be very aggressive at feeders to both other siskins and other species that are about their same size (goldfinches) or even a little larger (titmice). When being aggressive they assume a display called head-forward threat in which they lean forward, point their opened bill at the intruder, and may slightly raise their wings. The more crowded a feeder is, the more aggression there is for getting a perch from which to feed.

Head-forward threat is a common display by many species of birds and one of the most frequently seen at feeders. Other birds that give it are chickadees, titmice, finches, and goldfinches.

Here Again, Gone Again

It is difficult to say with certainty that you will always find pine siskins at a particular time of year in a particular spot, since pine siskins are irregular both in where they breed and where they winter. They seem to move around a great deal in response to the available food, remaining in one spot when it is plentiful and moving on when it is scarce. Therefore, in the East and Midwest, you may have lots of pine siskins at your feeder one year and possibly none the next.

Watching Pine Siskins Feed

Pine siskins are primarily seed eaters, favoring the seeds of conifers, birches, alders, eucalyptus, and a wide variety of weed seeds along roads and in fields. The birds are very adept at crawling out on fine branches or even hanging upside down to reach tree seeds. In spring they may also feed on tree flowers and the early seeds of maples or elms.

Several other feeding habits of pine siskins include gleaning insects such as aphids off tree leaves, eating the leaves and flowers off young plants, and occasionally even being garden pests by eating young vegetable shoots. Also, siskins from time to time are attracted to salt and ashes. This last habit has been noted by many people, especially in winter, when the birds are drawn to the salt used on roads to melt snow and ice.

Pine siskins seem to love hanging feeders or trays where there is either hulled sunflower or thistle. Like goldfinches, they tend to sit at one spot and feed continuously rather than take one seed at a time away from the feeder to eat it, like chickadees or titmice.

Siskin Sounds

Pine siskins have a flight call and flight pattern similar to that of their close cousin, the American goldfinch (the two species belong to the genus *Carduelis*). Their flight call is a three-syllable "ti-te-ti," and their flight is undulating. When flying, siskins tend to remain in a tight flock, fly quite high, and then drop down quickly when they land.

Pine siskin. A small brown-streaked bird with a fine pointed bill and touches of yellow on the wings and tail.

Pine siskin range map

Once a flock lands, it tends to be noisy, and the various calls used include an upward slurred whistle like that of the goldfinch, which sounds like "sweeet," and a distinctive call that will help you recognize the bird, which sounds like "zzzzzzz" and has been compared to escaping steam. It is a harsh call and given frequently.

You will also hear pine siskins sing. In late winter they sit in the tops of trees as a flock and sing continuously for several hours in the morning. Their songs are a jumble of chirps and "sweeet" notes, somewhat canary-like, interspersed with their harsh "zzzzzzz" sound. The function of this singing is unknown. It is interesting that this behavior is so similar to that of goldfinches in spring.

Siskins Pining for Each Other

Pine siskin courtship starts in January and February, while the birds are still in their winter flocks, and there are two aspects of their courtship that you may see. One is mate-finding, where the male takes food in his bill, flies to the female, and gives it to her. The female may crouch and flutter her wings when receiving food.

The other feature of courtship you may observe is a display flight by the male. Leaving from a perch near the female, he flies up in circles with tail spread and a rapid fluttering flight, singing continuously as he circles higher. Soon he stops circling and drops down to perch near the female. The flight may then be repeated.

Bird Feeder Journal

March 21, 11 A.M. A flock of about fifty pine siskins has arrived in our yard and found our hanging feeders with hulled sunflower seeds. There are too many to all feed at once, so the birds are very aggressive, pushing each other off perches. They are alternating periods of eating with periods of perching in the top of a nearby tree, singing and preening. Last year we saw no siskins at all!

May 9, 10 A.M. The siskins are still here, and we wonder how long they will stay before migrating to their northern breeding grounds. Have our well-stocked feeders kept them from migrating?

May 11, 2 P.M. The siskins seem to have left, for we did not see them yesterday or today. We will just have to wait till next year to enjoy them again.

RED-WINGED BLACKBIRD

Red-Winged Blackbird / *Agelaius phoeniceus*

Where's the Female?

The first time most people see a female red-wing they are sure that they have spotted a new species of bird. Because they are so familiar with the male, whose plumage accounts for the name of the whole species, they do not recognize the female as his mate, since she has neither black plumage nor a bright red patch on her wing but instead is streaked with brown. She looks a little like a large sparrow.

In spring, the males arrive first on the breeding grounds. Look for them each morning and afternoon on their territories in marshes where they most commonly breed. Within one to two weeks the females arrive, and then the marshes become a whirlwind of activity. Males defend territories more actively, as well as court and chase after females, and in some cases females are starting to build nests. If you keep your eye on the females, you may see one fly by with nesting material. Follow her and you may locate a nest.

Dictionary of Red-Wing Calls

"Okaleeee"—This is the most commonly heard sound made by the red-wing and is given only by the male. When he sings this song on his territory, he usually spreads his wings at the same time. (See description of songspread below.)

"Ch'ch'ch'chee chee chee"—This is the main sound of the female and is not given by the male.

"Check check"—This harsh, short call is given by both male and female when there is some disturbance. They usually flick their tail when giving it.

There are many other sounds red-wings make, and it is fun to listen for them and to try to distinguish between them.

Watching Male Red-Wing Behavior

Male red-wings have a language of gestures that you can learn and begin to understand. They use these gestures to communicate with each other at feeders and on their nesting territories. One of the most common behaviors is called songspread: The male arches forward, spreads his wings to the sides, and exposes the bright red epaulets on each wing. Songspread is usually directed at another male and is a sign of dominance. You can easily see it on the bird's territory and occasionally at your feeder.

In another behavior, look for two males perched near each other at a territorial border or at your feeder that are tilting their bills up in the air. This is called bill tilt and is a competitive display between two males, a kind of standoff helping them settle disputes over dominance without fighting.

Red-winged blackbird, male. A medium-sized black bird with a red-and-yellow epaulet on his wing. The red may be exposed or covered.

Red-winged blackbird, female. A medium-sized bird, heavily streaked with brown, that sometimes has faint pink or yellow on the throat. This female is at the nest.

Red-winged blackbird range map

Winter Roosting

Starting in fall and continuing through the winter and into spring, red-wings gather each night in large communal roosts, which are usually located in marshes or dense trees. You can see the birds heading for the roosts in late afternoon just before sundown, forming large trailing flocks that all converge on the roost site. They usually give "check" calls as they fly overhead.

It is especially fun to get near to the spot where they roost and see them arrive by the hundreds or thousands. We enjoy taking a rough census of the birds as they fly in to the roost, counting them by fives and tens and keeping track of the total number. The red-wings are often joined by other related species, such as brown-headed cowbirds, common grackles, and rusty blackbirds.

Watching Red-Wings Feed

Although red-wings are territorial, they may leave their territory for part of each day to feed elsewhere. In the marsh they feed on insects, but when they leave they may go to fields, where they feed on grains and seeds; this preference explains why they will come to your feeder. We find they like cracked corn and other smaller seeds. Like most birds, they feed their developing young primarily insects, for these are rich in protein.

Bird Feeder Journal

March 12, 10 A.M. Some of the first songs of red-wings can be heard from the field. It makes us think spring is here, but we have experienced this too many times to be fooled. The birds that are singing are just very early migrants, and there is still plenty of winter left.

June 13, 10 A.M. Every time we go out to check on the progress of our raspberry patch in the field, a male and female red-wing start flying about and giving their "check" call. They probably have a nest there.

June 15, 9 A.M. By following closely the actions of the female around the raspberry patch, we have found the nest! It is built out of grasses and woven around several stems in a clump of goldenrod. There are four baby birds in it with little bits of down all over them. After visiting the nest briefly we left and the parents continued feeding the young.

SPARROWS

Song Sparrow / *Melospiza melodia*   American Tree Sparrow / *Spizella arborea*

White-Throated Sparrow / *Zonotrichia albicollis*   Fox Sparrow / *Passerella iliaca*

White-Crowned Sparrow / *Zonotrichia leucophrys*

Little Brown Birds?

A lot of people refer to any type of sparrow as a little brown bird, probably assuming that to distinguish one species of sparrow from another is a job for only a dedicated birder or compulsive hairsplitter. But this is far from the truth. Many sparrows are easy to tell apart, and this includes the ones that regularly visit your feeder.

First of all, there are only five sparrows that are commonly seen at feeders (not including the house sparrow, which is not a real sparrow but a weaver finch). They are the American tree sparrow, song sparrow, fox sparrow, white-crowned sparrow, and white-throated sparrow.

To identify sparrows, look at the patterns on their breast and head. Three of these sparrows have clear, *unstreaked breasts*—the tree sparrow, white-throated sparrow, and white-crowned sparrow. They are easily distinguished from each other: The white-throated sparrow has an obvious white patch on its throat (also known as a bib), and its head is striped with black and white or tan and brown; the white-crowned sparrow is all grayish except for black and white stripes on its head; and the tree sparrow has a rusty cap and dark dot in the center of its clear breast.

The two other sparrows have *breasts streaked* with brown. Both also have a darker spot on their breast where some of the streaking is more dense. The song sparrow is a fairly dull brown, while the fox sparrow has a rusty red tail (in the East, rusty red all over) and is clearly larger than other sparrows.

Listen for Their Spring Songs

Even though the fox, tree, white-crowned, and white-throated sparrows do most of their singing on their breeding grounds—which are far to the north, and in the case of the white-crowned in the West—you may have a chance to hear each give its song at your feeder in late winter and spring before it starts to migrate.

The sparrow with the most easily recognized song is the white-throated sparrow. Its song is one or two clear whistles followed by three quavering whistles on a different pitch. Some people say it sounds like "pure, sweet Canada Canada Canada."

Song sparrow. A small brown bird with streaks on its breast and a central breast dot. The male and female look alike.

Song sparrow range map

White-throated sparrow, white-striped race. A small brown bird with an unstreaked breast, a white throat, and white and black stripes on its head; it also has yellow marks just above the bill. The male and female look alike.

White-throated sparrow range map

The songs of the other two that nest to the North are not as readily described and not as easily distinguished by the beginner. However, we encourage you to listen to them on a record (see the recordings listed in the chapter "Resources," p. 84) and then listen for them at your feeder in late winter.

The song sparrow is the one feeder sparrow that breeds all across the continent, and after being attracted to your feeder it may even nest in your yard. Its song is one short note repeated several times, followed by a series of warblings. Look for it singing from the top of a shrub or small tree as it announces its territory. It generally nests in open habitats, such as suburban areas and farmland.

Watching Sparrows Feed

It is fun to watch sparrows feed both at your feeder and in the wild. Most of our sparrows prefer to feed at ground or tray feeders, and they usually like some brushy cover nearby that they can dash into for protection. In the wild they love weed seeds and can be found in weedy fields or patches along roads and paths. This is particularly true of song sparrows and white-crowned sparrows.

Tree sparrows often feed above the ground, taking seeds directly off weeds and trees. They can be seen with goldfinches eating seeds off birches and alders. They also occasionally perch atop a weed and flutter their wings, causing seeds to fall out, and then drop down to feed on them. They have been seen to do this with the seeds of mullein, a common wildflower. They also often feed in trees above the ground, so they may very well visit one of your hanging feeders.

Fox sparrows and white-throated sparrows have a slightly different way of feeding. They take repeated short jumps forward and then backward, scraping away vegetation with their feet as they do so. This uncovers fallen seeds and possibly some insects under leaves and debris. Because of this method, they can also feed in forest edges and shrub borders where there are fallen leaves over the soil.

Winter Social Behavior

Most of the sparrows you see in winter are on their wintering grounds, their Florida vacation, as it were. Just as you might go to the same place for vacation several times, so do the sparrows tend to return to the same wintering spot each year. Thus, of the sparrows that you see at your feeder, many of the older ones may have been there before.

In winter, each species of sparrow has a slightly different social arrangement. The song and fox sparrows tend to be seen alone or in small, loose

White-throated sparrow, tan-striped race. A small brown bird with an unstreaked breast, a white throat, beige and brown stripes on the head, and faint yellow marks above bill. The male and female look alike.

White-crowned sparrow. A small grayish bird with an unstreaked breast and bold black and white stripes on its head. There is no yellow above the bill and no white on the throat, as in the similar white-throated sparrow. The male and female look alike.

White-crowned sparrow range map

flocks of several birds. These species generally stay in the same area all winter. Song sparrow males may even remain on their breeding territories and leave only when there is a shortage of food.

Tree sparrows form large flocks of about fifty birds that seem to roam over a large area, taking advantage of the local abundance of tree seeds. These flocks may break up into smaller groups that remain more closely associated throughout winter. All the tree sparrows in a given area may be organized into a hierarchy.

White-throated sparrows tend to feed in small flocks of five to ten birds that stay in shrubbery and other dense cover. White-crowned sparrows have been studied quite carefully, and they have been found to stay in large flocks of twenty-five to fifty birds. In some cases these flocks have a fairly fixed membership throughout the winter and remain in a defined area which does not overlap that of other white-crowned sparrow flocks. Although each flock seems to have its own "turf," there is no aggression between flocks to suggest active territorial defense.

Within a flock of white-crowned sparrows there is often competition for food. You may see one run at another and displace it, or two birds facing each other may flutter a short distance into the air. These are signs of competition and aggression, which indicate that the flocks may have a hierarchy.

Look for all these patterns of behavior both in the wild and at your feeder.

Fox sparrow. A small to medium-sized red-brown bird with heavy reddish streaking on its breast and sometimes a central breast dot. The wings and tail are often quite reddish. The male and female look alike. This is the largest of the sparrows.

Fox sparrow range map

Bird Feeder Journal

November 11, 9 A.M. Our first tree sparrows and juncos have arrived today. Will they fly farther south or will they be our winter residents? With their arrival at our ground feeder, winter has officially started.

March 12, 4 P.M. Three fox sparrows at the feeder! They are the first we have seen this winter. They look so big and red compared with other sparrows. They must be migrating north. Last year we also had three fox sparrows at this same time; could it be that they are the same ones?

March 20, 8:30 A.M. It is a clear morning with a break in the cold. We have just heard the beautiful song of the fox sparrows, and the white-throated sparrows are singing throughout the woods. We wonder why they start singing while on migration.

April 20, 10 A.M. Our resident male song sparrow is at the ground feeder chasing off all small birds. It has lunged at white-throated sparrows, juncos, and other song sparrows. It is alternating this with going to the brush pile and singing. These are the first signs of this year's territorial behavior.

Tree sparrow. A small brown bird with an unstreaked breast that has a central dot. The male and female look alike.

American tree sparrow range map

STARLING

European Starling / *Sturnus vulgaris*

Changing Colors

One of the most amazing things about starlings is how much they change in appearance over the winter. After going through their yearly molt of all the feathers in late summer, they have a dark bill and black plumage speckled all over with small white V's. By spring, the white tips of their feathers have worn off, leaving the birds totally dark and iridescent, especially on their head and neck.

At this time their bill also changes from dark to light, and in the case of the males, to bright yellow. At the end of breeding, the birds have their annual molt, in which they acquire their speckled plumage and their bill turns dark again. Look for these changes in the starlings near you.

How to Recognize Juveniles

Young starlings from the year's first brood begin to be independent of their parents by early summer. You can recognize them by their plumage and their behavior. They are the same size as their parents but are dark brown and have dark bills. They keep this plumage until they molt in late summer along with the adults. After this molt the adults and young birds look identical.

Young starlings, as soon as they are independent, join other young starlings in flocks that can be seen feeding together on lawns and along highways. You will not see adults feeding in groups in summer, for they are still raising more broods. However, when they finish breeding in late summer, they join the juveniles, and they all feed together.

Nighttime Gatherings

Most people do not know about starling roosting habits unless they live near a roost site. Roosts are places where starlings gather for the night, in numbers ranging from a few hundred to a few hundred thousand. Roosts are located in protected spots, such as marshes or in groves of trees; in the city they are often located on the ledges beneath large bridges.

Every evening just before sundown the birds start to fly in to the roost from outlying areas, sometimes 10 or more miles away. Along their route they often stop in the tops of trees and gather with other flocks of starlings. At these stopovers the birds call noisily, periodically flying up into the air and then settling again.

The final flight to the roost is fascinating — you will see large flocks circling above the spot and then diving with great speed into the roost. The roost is noisy, often long into the night.

No one knows exactly why birds roost together,

European starling, adult, in spring and summer. A medium-sized black bird with iridescence on its head and neck and a yellow bill. The male and female look similar.

especially in such large numbers. Some of the newest theories propose that roosts provide some protection from predators and that they are close to alternative sources of food that the birds can exploit on their way to and from their daily centers of activity.

Watching Starlings Feed

In the wild, starlings often feed in flocks. In fall you can see a flock descend on a shrub in fruit, pick it clean in a few minutes, and then fly off. Starlings also feed on insects in grassy areas and are important predators of insect pests such as cutworm and Japanese beetle larvae, grasshoppers, and other insects found in fields or lawns. Because of this, starlings can be very beneficial.

At the feeder, starlings are attracted to suet, white millet, peanut hearts, and, to a lesser extent, striped sunflower seed. Many people find starlings objectionable at their feeders, for they are aggressive and seem to scare off other birds. One way to counteract this is to lessen the competition by adding feeders in varying spots around your yard.

"Startling" Introduction

Most of our common feeder birds are native to the continent, but a few have been introduced by humans from other parts of the world. The starling is one of our introduced species. Sixty pairs were first released into Central Park in New York City in 1890, and they began to breed that same year in the crannies of buildings. The next year another forty pairs were released in the same area. A mere fifty years after that, starlings had spread to almost every part of the United States and southern Canada. They are one of nature's remarkable success stories and an amazing lesson on how far-reaching a simple act of human intervention in nature can be.

Watching Starling Behavior

Starling behavior is particularly fascinating in spring when males start to defend nest holes by spending much of each day perched near the hole on a branch.

When another male comes nearby, the defending male may perform several interesting behaviors. First, it may do crowing, a chortling sound given with the bill closed, head tilted up, and throat feathers ruffled out, or the defender may fluff out its feathers or wipe its bill back and forth over a branch.

European starling in fall and winter. A medium-sized black bird with white dots on its breast and a dark bill.

European starling range map

When a female flies near, the male will do a behavior called rowing, in which it rotates its wings in a rowing manner and calls loudly, possibly trying to attract the female's attention to himself and his nest hole.

Bird Feeder Journal

May 5, 10 A.M. There are young starlings feeding in a flock on the short grass area of our field. We can tell they are fledglings by their calls and brownish color. It is hard to believe that the adults have already completed one brood; many other species have not even arrived for the summer.

June 5, 8 A.M. There are starlings peering into the nest boxes in our field. Our swallow colony, which uses the boxes, is very upset and is swirling about the starlings. Luckily, the box openings are 1½ inches in diameter and just a little too small for the starlings to enter. After about a half hour of trying, the starlings give up.

TITMOUSE

Tufted Titmouse / *Parus bicolor*

A Mouse with a Tuft?

One of the liveliest birds that come to our feeders is the tufted titmouse. Some people wonder if the name "titmouse" has anything to do with mice. Actually, "mouse" comes from the Anglo-Saxon word "mase," which meant a kind of bird, and "tit" is from the old Icelandic word for small. The "tuft" refers to the longer feathers, or crest, on its head, which the bird can raise or lower, reflecting its emotional state. When the crest is raised, the bird may be more competitive or combative; when lowered, the bird may either be more at ease or fearful.

The titmouse's nearest relative at the feeder is the chickadee. In fact, both birds are in the genus *Parus*, and their relatedness is apparent in their behavior. They have similar nesting and breeding habits and calls, and when they come to the feeder, both have the tendency to take one seed, fly away, eat it, and then return for the next.

Winter Society

Every species of bird has some kind of social arrangement during winter. Some remain as lone individuals, some form pairs, some are loose roaming flocks, and others are stable flocks that stay in open areas. Generally, titmice fall into this last category, remaining through winter as a family group of three to six birds on a fixed range of about 15 to 20 acres. Groups seem to be composed of parents and young; however, only a few studies with banded birds in winter have been done, so with further study more facts about their winter society may come to light.

Throughout winter you can see this flock visit your feeder. When you see one bird, there will be several others nearby or on their way. If you can remember the number of birds in the flock, you can tell whether you have more than one flock at your feeder.

First Signs of Breeding Behavior

The behavior of titmouse flocks undergoes a change in late winter: Members of the flock will chase each other and give lots of scolding calls. This signals the beginning of the breeding period. The flocks are breaking up, and individual birds are starting to defend territories. In most cases it is probably the younger birds that are forced to leave and find their own areas in which to breed.

At the same time you may hear male titmice give their song that sounds like "peer peer peer" as they define their territory to other males and advertise their presence to females in the area. Singing by two neighboring males early in the season may bring them together at a common border, where they may chase each other or fight as they better define the border.

Soon after this you can see the most obvious feature of titmouse courtship — mate-feeding. The male gets food (possibly from your feeder), carries it to the female, and places it in her bill. Meanwhile the female usually quivers her wings and gives a continuous, high-pitched whistle that sounds like "seee seee seee seee," a little like a whistling teapot. It is so high-pitched that it can be hard to hear. Wing-quivering and high-pitched calls can also occur in aggressive encounters between males.

Dictionary of Titmouse Calls

"Peer peer" or "peter peter" — This series of clear, down-slurred whistles constitutes titmouse song. It is given mostly by males from late winter into early summer, although occasionally it is given softly by the female as she approaches the nest with food. If you imitate this call, a male will often come close to investigate.

"Tseep" — This is a high, short sound given between a pair or members of a flock as a contact call. It helps them keep in aural contact while they use their eyes to look for food.

Tufted titmouse. A small gray bird with a crest. The male and female look alike.

Tufted titmouse range map

"Jway jway jway" — This is a scolding call given during any disturbance, including your presence near the feeder.

"Seee" — This is an extremely high-pitched, rapidly repeated call given during mate-feeding or aggressive encounters between males.

Nesting and Juveniles

Tufted titmice nest in tree holes such as knotholes or old woodpecker homes. If you want these birds nesting in your area, put up bird boxes and leave up old dead trees. In late May and early June you may see the first fledglings flying about with their parents. They can be distinguished from the parents all summer by the lack of a black patch on their forehead; they also continually fly after the parents, giving a "seee-jweee" call as they beg for food. After their annual molt in late summer, they get the black patch on their forehead and look just like the adults.

Rare Bird?

Before 1955 the tufted titmouse was considered a rare bird in New England and most other northern states. If one was sighted, people would travel many miles to see it, but since then it has become quite common from southeastern Minnesota to southern Ontario and southern New England. Along with the northern cardinal and northern mockingbird, it has been expanding its range. This may be in part due to the increasing use of bird feeders in northern areas, enabling the birds to survive through the winter.

Bird Feeder Journal

March 29, 9 A.M. The titmice are building a nest in the bird box we put up on the old cedar tree. We can see them from our study window as they make trips with nesting material.

March 30, 9:30 A.M. We saw the titmouse hopping over the blanket our dog lies on at our front step. As we watched, it collected dog hairs in its bill and took them to the nest box, probably as a soft inner lining.

April 10, 2 P.M. A female titmouse is quivering her wings and giving the high "seee" call as she sits on our waiting perch next to the feeder. The male is at the sunflower feeder and is making trips to feed her, a good sign that their courtship is under way.

TOWHEE

Rufous-Sided Towhee / *Pipilo erythrophthalmus*

Red-Eyed Chirper

The scientific name of the towhee is *Pipilo erythrophthalmus,* which is practically impossible to pronounce but interesting in translation. It means "red-eyed chirper" and refers to the red eye of the bird and its most common call, a short sound variously described as "chewink," "towhee," or "joreee." "Chewink" is, in fact, another common name for towhees. This common call is slightly different in the West, where it sounds more like the meow of a cat, but in East and West the call seems to be used to help a mated pair keep in contact as they move about the dense underbrush, where they nest.

The song of the towhee is aptly described as "drink your tea" and is given only by the male. The last part of the song is a long, trilling "eee" sound and in some cases is the only part of the song that is given. It can be heard throughout the year but most often in spring and summer when the male is defining a territory and attracting a mate.

The "chewink" call and song may be your only indication that towhees are in your area, for the birds often stay in dense brush and shrubbery, making them hard to see.

Watching Towhees Feed

Towhees feed almost exclusively on the ground. Their feeding behavior is similar to that of the white-throated sparrow in that they hop forward and then quickly jump backward, dragging their feet as they do so. This scraping backward pulls away leaves and debris from the soil surface and at the same time reveals insects and seeds below. The birds then feed in these exposed areas. A towhee on a platform feeder will still scrape in this manner even though seeds are visible, and this has the effect of scattering all of the seed off the platform.

Towhees eat primarily seeds and berries, but in spring and summer insects found on the ground compose about half their diet. Of all feeders they will be most attracted to your ground feeder, and then only if there is underbrush and other cover very nearby. They are usually shy at feeders and dive into cover at the slightest disturbance.

Hidden Breeding Behavior

If you hear towhees in your yard in spring and summer, chances are they are nesting there. Male towhees usually arrive first; they will sing and defend a territory of about 1½ to 2 acres. Two changes in behavior will alert you to the arrival of a female and its pairing with the male. The male will stop singing, and you will hear the "chewink" call given back and forth between the pair.

The female does all building of the nest, which is placed on the ground, usually under the bough of a tree or shrub. It is hard to locate the nest, since the female rarely flies directly to it; instead, she lands on a perch a few feet away and then walks to it along the ground and under cover.

Rufous-sided towhee, male. A medium-sized bird with a black head, wings, back, and tail, and rufous sides.

Rufous-sided towhee, female. A medium-sized bird with a brown head, wings, back, and tail, and rufous sides.

Rufous-sided towhee range map

Occasionally parent towhees will bring their young to a feeder area, and you can see the whole family.

Flock Behavior

On their wintering grounds towhees often form loose flocks containing as many as twenty-five birds. They range over an area of 20 to 30 acres, and they may join with flocks of other species, such as cardinals.

The spring migration is made in small flocks, which upon arrival at the breeding grounds stay together for a few days before individual males leave for their own territories. In late summer, after breeding, juveniles may also join small flocks before migration.

Male/Female, Western/Eastern

The appearance of the towhee varies in different parts of the country. Towhees in the East have dark heads and backs, rufous sides, a white belly, and a red eye. Towhees in the West are similar except that they also have white spots on their dark wings and back. In the Southeast there is a race of towhees with a white rather than a red eye. Not too long ago the western form was called the spotted towhee and believed to be a separate species. Now the eastern and western forms are known to interbreed and so are considered one species.

The differences between males and females also vary from East to West. They are more pronounced in the East, where the head, back, wings, and tail of the female are a rich brown, while those of the male are black. In the West the female plumage is brown-black or gray-black and closer to the pure black of the male.

Bird Feeder Journal

April 7, 9:30 A.M. A male towhee is giving his "drink-your-tea" song from within our woods. He must have arrived on the weather front that came through last night, for there also seem to be other new birds in the yard. For several years we have had a male stop and sing for a few days but then move on. Maybe this one will stay.

April 29, 10 A.M. A pair of towhees is building a nest at the edge of our woods! We have seen the female collecting leaves and carrying them in her bill, but we have not yet located the nest's exact whereabouts. We look forward to following the pair's behavior through their breeding cycle.

WOODPECKERS

Downy Woodpecker / *Picoides pubescens*

Hairy Woodpecker / *Picoides villosus*

Red-Bellied Woodpecker / *Melanerpes carolinus*

Woodpeckers That Visit Feeders

Although there are about twenty species of woodpeckers that live in North America, only a few of them are widespread and regularly come to feeders. The hairy and downy both live throughout the continent and will come to suet feeders, although the downy seems less shy about it. The red-bellied woodpecker lives in only the eastern half of North America but is a bold woodpecker that loves suburban areas and readily visits feeders.

Who's Downy? Who's Hairy?
Who's Red-Bellied?

The names give no clues on how to tell these species of woodpeckers apart. The downy and hairy look almost identical, but neither seems downy or hairy. There are, however, several ways to distinguish between them. The first is size. The downy is the smaller bird, being about 7 inches long, while the hairy is a little over 9 inches long. But with nothing to compare the bird to, the size of the bird you are watching is difficult to determine.

A better way to tell them apart is by the size of their bill in proportion to their head. The downy bill is short, less than half the depth of the bird's head, while the hairy bill is long and more than half the depth of its head.

One other subtle difference that you may be able to see when the bird is close by at your feeder is that the outer white tail feathers of the downy are often barred with black, and those of the hairy are all white.

The name of the red-bellied woodpecker makes even less sense, for the only red it has is on its head. This woodpecker looks very different from the other two, having a lighter back and no black-and-white markings on its head.

Distinguishing Females from Males

In both the hairy and downy woodpeckers it is quite easy to tell a male from a female. The male has a red spot at the back of his head; the female has no red on her head. When the male is involved in an aggressive interaction with another male, he may raise the feathers on the back of his head, making the red patch stand out boldly.

Both male and female red-bellied woodpeckers have red on their heads, but to different degrees. The red on the female is limited to the back of her head, whereas the red on the male extends from the back of his head all the way over the top to the base of his bill.

Recognizing Individual Woodpeckers

With most birds, individuals of the same species and same sex look very similar, but with hairy and downy woodpeckers it is quite possible to recognize individual birds. This is because the patterns of black and white on the back of the female's head and the patterns of red, black, and white on the back of the male's head vary greatly among individuals. We keep a little notebook in which we roughly sketch the pattern on the back of the head for individuals that come to our feeder. In this way we keep track of how many male and female downies and hairies come to our feeder and live on our property.

How Many Woodpeckers
Live Near You?

Most woodpeckers live all year in the same area and do not migrate. They also tend to stay with or near their mate through the year, although in winter they are more loosely associated. Therefore, if your feeder is in the middle of a hairy or downy home range, you will probably have only one pair of each showing up at your feeder. You may, however, be at the edge of two or more home ranges and thus have two or, rarely, three pairs around. If you identify the individuals using their head patterns, you can tell how many pairs you have.

Downies and hairies live peacefully in the same area, occasionally even nesting in the same tree, but neither is tolerant of others of the same species in its home range. This is particularly true during the breeding season, when each will chase others of its own species away.

Red-bellied woodpeckers may migrate to south of where they breed, especially those breeding at the northern limit of their range. This may cause a greater concentration of red-bellies farther south in winter.

Pecking Versus Drumming

Woodpeckers make two different kinds of sounds with their bills. One is a soft, irregular pecking; the other is a loud, rapid drumming occurring in bursts of one to two seconds.

The irregular *pecking* is the sound the bill makes when the woodpecker is searching for food or excavating a nest hole. During this pecking, wood is actually chipped away. The pecking is a quiet sound and not often heard. The loud, rapid *drumming* is done by male or female woodpeckers on resonant surfaces. It is really a signal, like song in other birds, that announces the bird's presence on its territory to its mate or competitors. When the bird does this, no wood is chipped away. The birds pick any resonant spot; it may be some part of your house, such as a drainpipe or gutter.

If a woodpecker *drums* on your house, it does not mean that you have termites, and generally it will not damage your house. Drumming is heard only during the breeding season (late winter to midsummer), and the first drumming is a good sign that the breeding cycle for woodpeckers has begun.

If a woodpecker is *pecking* on your house and chipping away wood, it is likely that there are insects at the spot. If you get rid of the insects, the woodpeckers will stop. Pecking, unlike drumming, can be heard at any time of year.

Watching Woodpeckers Feed

At your feeder, woodpeckers are especially attracted to suet, but they will also come to feeders

Downy woodpecker, male. A small bird with black and white markings on the wings and head, white on the back and belly. The male has a red patch on the back of his head. The male hairy woodpecker looks similar but has a longer bill and larger body.

Downy woodpecker range map

that have sunflower seed, preferably hulled. Downies seem less shy than hairies and come more readily to feeders near our house.

In the wild, woodpeckers primarily eat insects, such as ants and the larvae of wood-boring beetles, which they uncover by pecking away bits of wood and bark. The hairy and downy probably are able to

Hairy woodpecker female on left, downy woodpecker female on right. The females are similar to the males but lack the red patch on the back of the head.

Hairy woodpecker range map

live peacefully in the same areas because their size difference allows them to take advantage of different food sources. The downy eats smaller insects that it finds just under the bark surface, and after it has pecked at a tree you can hardly see the marks left behind. The hairy, with its larger bill, digs deeper into the wood for a different set of insects, and you can always see chips out of the wood where it has fed.

The reason the red-bellied can coexist with the downy and hairy is probably that its eating habits are slightly different than theirs. It will feed on insects in the ground, and it eats a great deal of fruit as well. In fact, it is known for pecking on oranges in the South. Occasionally the red-bellied will drink at sap from sapsucker holes made in trees, and it is also known for storing bits of food — such as nuts or insects — in bark crevices or other crannies.

Nest Holes

Woodpeckers are among the few birds that can create their own nest holes. Most other hole-nesting species depend on holes previously made by woodpeckers. The downy, with its shorter bill, always chooses dead wood in which to excavate; the red-bellied woodpecker may use either live or dead wood; the hairy, with its larger and more powerful bill, almost always excavates in live wood.

You can distinguish between the holes of these three woodpeckers by the size of the entrance. Downy entrance holes are about 1¼ inches in diameter; red-bellied entrances are about 1¾ to 2¼ inches in diameter; and hairy entrance holes tend to be slightly oval, about 2 inches wide and 2½ inches high.

If you want downies nesting in your yard, then be sure to leave plenty of dead stubs in your trees;

otherwise they will have no place to excavate. In addition, the dead wood provides places for all species to feed on insects. Holes made during the breeding season also may be used as roost holes during winter. And in the following year other species of birds, such as chickadees, titmice, or nuthatches, will use them to nest in.

Bird Feeder Journal

February 2, 11:30 A.M. Two male downies are at the hanging feeder eating hulled sunflower seeds. They seem disturbed at each other's presence. They are giving "queek-queek" calls, chasing each other around the tree trunk, and at one point one hangs upside down under the feeder in a threat posture, its wings held in a **V** and its tail fully spread. A spectacular display.

August 12, 1 P.M. An adult downy and an immature downy have just shown up at the suet feeder. The adult looks incredibly ragged with its feathers all worn; it may even be starting to molt. There is probably a lot of wear on its feathers as it goes in and out of its nest hole to care for the young. In contrast, the immature bird has perfect plumage, with a clear white breast and bold markings on the back — a sign of the leisure of youth!

Red-bellied woodpecker, male. A medium-sized bird with black and white bars on its back, grayish underparts. The male has red extending from the back of his head to the base of his bill. The female has red only on the back of her head (see p. 27).

Red-bellied woodpecker range map

RESOURCES

This is a selective list of what we think are the best resources for furthering your knowledge of attracting, identifying, and understanding birds.

Attracting Birds

John V. Dennis, *A Complete Guide to Bird Feeding.* New York: Alfred A. Knopf, 1981.

George H. Harrison, *The Backyard Bird Watcher.* New York: Simon and Schuster, 1979.

Stephen W. Kress, *The Audubon Society Guide to Attracting Birds.* New York: Charles Scribner's Sons, 1985.

John K. Terres, *Songbirds in Your Garden.* New York: Hawthorn Books, 1977.

Bird Behavior

Donald W. Stokes, *A Guide to Bird Behavior,* vol. I; Donald W. Stokes and Lillian Q. Stokes, *A Guide to Bird Behavior,* vol. II. Boston: Little, Brown and Co., 1979 and 1983, respectively.

Volume I birds: the American goldfinch, American kestrel, American robin, black-capped chickadee, blue jay, Canada goose, chimney swift, common crow, common flicker, common grackle, common yellowthroat, eastern kingbird, gray catbird, hairy woodpecker, herring gull, house sparrow, house wren, mallard, mockingbird, pigeon, red-eyed vireo, red-winged blackbird, song sparrow, starling, and tree sparrow.

Volume II birds: the barn swallow, belted kingfisher, brown-headed cowbird, brown thrasher, cardinal, cedar waxwing, chipping sparrow, downy woodpecker, eastern meadowlark, eastern phoebe, field sparrow, indigo bunting, killdeer, marsh wren, mourning dove, rose-breasted grosbeak, rufous-sided towhee, scarlet tanager, spotted sandpiper, tufted titmouse, white-breasted nuthatch, wood pewee, wood thrush, and yellow warbler.

Bird Identification

Roger Tory Peterson, ed., *A Field Guide to the Birds.* Boston: Houghton Mifflin Co., 1980.

Shirley L. Scott, ed. *A Field Guide to the Birds of North America.* Washington, D.C.: Geographic Society, 1983.

Feeder Supplies (catalogues available)

Aspects, P.O. Box 9, Bristol, RI 02809. Feeders.

Audubon Workshop, Inc., 1501 Paddock Drive, Northbrook, IL 60062. Feeders, seed.

Bird 'n' Hand Inc., 73 Sawyer Passway, Fitchburg, MA 01420. Feeders, seed.

The Brown Company, P.O. Box 277, Yawgoo Pond Road, West Kingston, RI 02892. Feeders.

The Crow's Nest Bookshop, Laboratory of Ornithology at Cornell University, 159 Sapsucker Woods Road, Ithaca, NY 14850. Feeders.

Droll Yankees, Inc., Mill Road, Foster, RI 02825. Feeders.

Duncraft, 33 Fisherville Road, Penacook, NH 03303. Feeders, seed.

Hummingbird Haven, 1255 Carmel Drive, Simi Valley, CA 93065. Hummingbird feeders.

Hyde Bird Feeder Company, 56 Felton Street, P.O. Box 168, Waltham, MA 02254. Feeders, seed.

Kaytee Products Inc., Chilton, WI 53014. Seed.

K-Feeders Enterprises, Inc., 4635 Post Road, Warwick, RI 02886. Feeders.

Nelson Manufacturing Company, 3049 12th Street, S.W., Cedar Rapids, IA 52404. Birdbath heaters.

Noel's Bird Feeders, Inc., Northwood, NH 03261. Feeders.

Perky-Pet Products, Inc., 2201 S. Wabash Street, Denver, CO 80231. Hummingbird feeders.

Stanford Seed, R.R. 1, Box 405, Denver, PA 17517. "Lyric" brand seed.

Wagner Products, P.O. Box 61, Farmingdale, NY 11735. Seed.

Magazines

Bird Watcher's Digest, P.O. Box 110, Marietta, OH 45750. A bimonthly magazine filled with interesting articles on birds, feeders, bird trips, and birding equipment. [Regular column by Donald and Lillian Stokes called "The Behavior-watcher's Notebook" in which they teach about behavior and answer readers' questions.]

The Living Bird Quarterly, Laboratory of Ornithology at Cornell University, 159 Sapsucker Woods Road, Ithaca, NY 14850. A quarterly magazine with fine photos and excellent articles on birds and birding around the world. [Includes a column by Donald and Lillian Stokes on watching bird behavior.]

Recordings of Songs and Calls

A Field Guide to Bird Songs Cassette. Peterson Field Guide Series. Laboratory of Ornithology at Cornell University.

Audible Audubon, 1977. This is a small battery-operated machine that comes with individual cards for each bird; you place the card into the machine to hear the bird's call or song. An easy way to compare songs.

YOUR BIRD FEEDER JOURNAL

We have provided this space to enhance your bird feeder experience. We see so many fascinating things at our feeders that it is hard to remember them all or to compare one event with another that may have happened much earlier. Therefore we keep a notebook and pencil right by our feeders at all times. This way it is easy to jot down the things that interest us. In the case of visual displays, we also try to make a sketch of what it looked like.

We find that looking back over our notes and sketches is extremely rewarding, helping us remember the tremendous variety of things that we have experienced. We encourage all of you to keep your own personal journal of the things you see at your feeder.

Why Keep Notes?

Besides being fun and helping you remember, keeping notes has some other important advantages. One is that it makes you look more closely and think more carefully about what you see. When you decide to make a note of something, you have to ask yourself, "What really did happen?"

Another important benefit of recording behavior at your feeder is that there is still a great deal to be learned about the lives of these birds. In many of the chapters about the individual birds we have pointed out areas of behavior that are still not understood. When it comes right down to it, it is amazing how little is known about the common things in nature that we see every day. You may see things that have never been seen before; by recording them, you may be contributing to scientific knowledge.

What Should You Record?

The best answer to this is: anything that catches your attention and interests you. You may want to look at feeding habits, bathing habits, social interactions, breeding behavior, migration timing, or any other part of a bird's life that occurs at or near your feeder.

How to Record

In the following pages we have included headings for the date, time of day, and the name of the bird. These are the first things to record. Under the heading "Observation," jot down a few notes about what you saw. Keep this book near your feeders with a pencil or pen handy so that you can quickly look up a bird, learn about its behavior, and record something you see.

Date _____   Time _____   Species _____

Observation

Date _____ Time _____ Species _____

Observation

Date _____ Time _____ Species _____

Observation

Date _____ Time _____ Species _____

Observation

Date _____ Time _____ Species _____

Observation

Date ——————— Time ——————— Species —————————————————

Observation

Date ——————— Time ——————— Species —————————————————

Observation

Date ——————— Time ——————— Species —————————————————

Observation

Date ——————— Time ——————— Species —————————————————

Observation

Date _____ Time _____ Species _____
Observation

Date _____ Time _____ Species _____
Observation

Date _____ Time _____ Species _____
Observation

Date _____ Time _____ Species _____
Observation

Date _____ Time _____ Species _____
Observation

Date _____ Time _____ Species _____
Observation

Date _____ Time _____ Species _____
Observation

Date _____ Time _____ Species _____
Observation